THE SOFT SCIENCE OF ROAD RACING MOTORCYCLES

THE SOFT SCIENCE OF ROAD RACING MOTORCYCLES

The Technical Procedures and Workbook for Road Racing Motorcycles

by Keith Code

First Edition

CODE BREAK

Acknowledgements

Editorial Advice and Assistance
Michael Church
Dylan Code
Cort Sutton
Judy Code
Tony Cohan

Help and Encouragement
Motorcyclist Magazine; Good guys.
Wayne Rainey; World champion.
Freddie Spencer; Answered questions.
Kenny Roberts; Said it was easy.
Rich Gilbert; Knows stuff.
L. Ron Hubbard; How to survive.
Rom Lovil; Said yes.
Mike Vaughan; Seconded the motion.
Dick Davis; There's more here than meets the eye.

Couldn't Have Done It Without 'Em
Judy Code
Dylan Code
My big sister, Audrey.
My Mom

Design and Illustration
The Spencer Bros.; Texans in So. Cal.

Photography
Mitch Boehm, ix
Rich Chenet, page 156
Dylan Code, pages 51, 52, 55, Back Cover
Blaine Covert, page 115
Richard Davis, Back cover
Ward McKee, Back cover
Manfred Mothes, pages 66, 100
Dick Raczuk, page 124
Tom Riles, Page 78
Sport Graphics, page 76, 78, 127
Leo Vogelzang, page 132

California Superbike School, Inc.
PO Box 9294
Glendale, CA 91226
800 530-3350

Printed in the United States of America

Warning: The riding techniques contained in this book are intended for racing purposes only. The author and publisher accept no responsibility for any accidents resulting in bodily harm or property damage that might occur fromn the increased speeds and rider ability that may be gained by the use of this material. The author and publisher do not guarantee that readers will attain the same high degree of riding skills that others have by applying these techniques. Supplemental notes and endorsements by Wayne Rainey should not be taken as any guarantee as to safety or competency that might be gained, but merely as personal experience. If expert assistance is required, the services of a state licensed agency should be sought.

Always wear proper protective clothing and observe local speed laws.

Dedication
To motorcycle riders and racers everywhere. Still free to taste danger.

CONTENTS

Margin notes by Wayne Rainey.

Author's Note

Since 1981 when I started **"A Twist Of The Wrist,"** a lot of laps have been run around lots of race tracks. That book was a broad stroke on the subject of motorcycle riding technology. This one is an even more detailed view of going fast.

I would like to be able to say that the whole subject is covered in **"A Twist"** and **"Soft Science,"** but it isn't. There's more to it yet. Having 7,000 students through the **Superbike School**, and working with six factory riders plus a few other good racers, has shown me a lot.

Each rider, myself included, has his own way of fitting all the thoughts and ideas about road racing into his riding. **How** you do it is very personal. **What** you are dealing with is the same for everyone. For instance, it is obvious that world class riders think very differently about the subject of traction. But, it is still the subject of traction. And you can understand it.

One year ago I thought I had **"Soft Science"** completed, but I needed to test the material before putting it out in book form. I called up some of California's best club level riders and held a seminar. The seminar was 10 hours of instruction straight from the information I had written down.

The results were impressive. The fast guys went even faster. The times were so good, they were protested for illegal engines! The second level fast guys went two to three seconds faster. The most mediocre result was that the rider was able to run his previous fastest times consistently and with ease. I was enthusiastic, but felt something was still missing.

I spent another year on the book, re-did the seminars, had some of the same riders back one year later, got the same kind of results as before, and now it's over to you. It works!

When I approached Wayne Rainey to do some notes for the book, I wanted to have a good name connected with this work. From a publishing point of view, it would certainly help sell copies. Wayne came to my home and read through a few chapters. He liked the material. It was of use to him and he was sure it would be to others. He became very excited about the whole project and it really made me feel great to get that response from a world class rider. It made the hundreds of hours of work worthwhile.

Use it.

Keith Code

Things that take a lot of attention you may forget about, until you are back on the track. This book reminds you of those things so they can be fixed before the track.

1

Tricks Or Tools?

If your intention is to improve, not just pick up some "tricks," you should understand exactly what is going on with the most important part of the riding package, the rider. After all, whether your bike works well or not is measured in ten/thousandths of inches and millimeters, that's how far machine technology has come. By comparison, rider technology is still lagging behind.

It is very difficult to put a micrometer on the rider's main tool, his **ideas** of how to do the riding. This book is designed to help you do that job. **By using the checklists and questionnaires, you can probe your own ideas and measure them**.

Measure Yourself

It's good to have a goal, a lot of riders don't have one. I had one at Mid-Ohio last year and after I hit the track record went 3 seconds faster.

It is important for you to set a **target for improvement** at each practice session or race meeting. The most obvious and easiest measure of your improvement is lap times. A better lap time or a better lap time average for a group of laps is a sure indication that what you are doing is working. You are setting a "target" lap time to give yourself an exact goal for improvement.

Setting a target lap time for a session that is 5 seconds faster than you ever went before would probably be a bad idea. Setting a target of 1 second faster for each race would be real enough for most riders. As you become faster, your target will be smaller.

Take Small Bites

If you run two practices and two races in a day and times are 1 second better, you are doing a good job. If you are 5 seconds off the winning pace it would only take you 5 race meetings to get in with the fast guys.

From an improvement point of view, you only have to go ¼ second faster each practice and each race to make your **target!** Once you are in range of winning lap times your **target** may be ¼ second for the whole day.

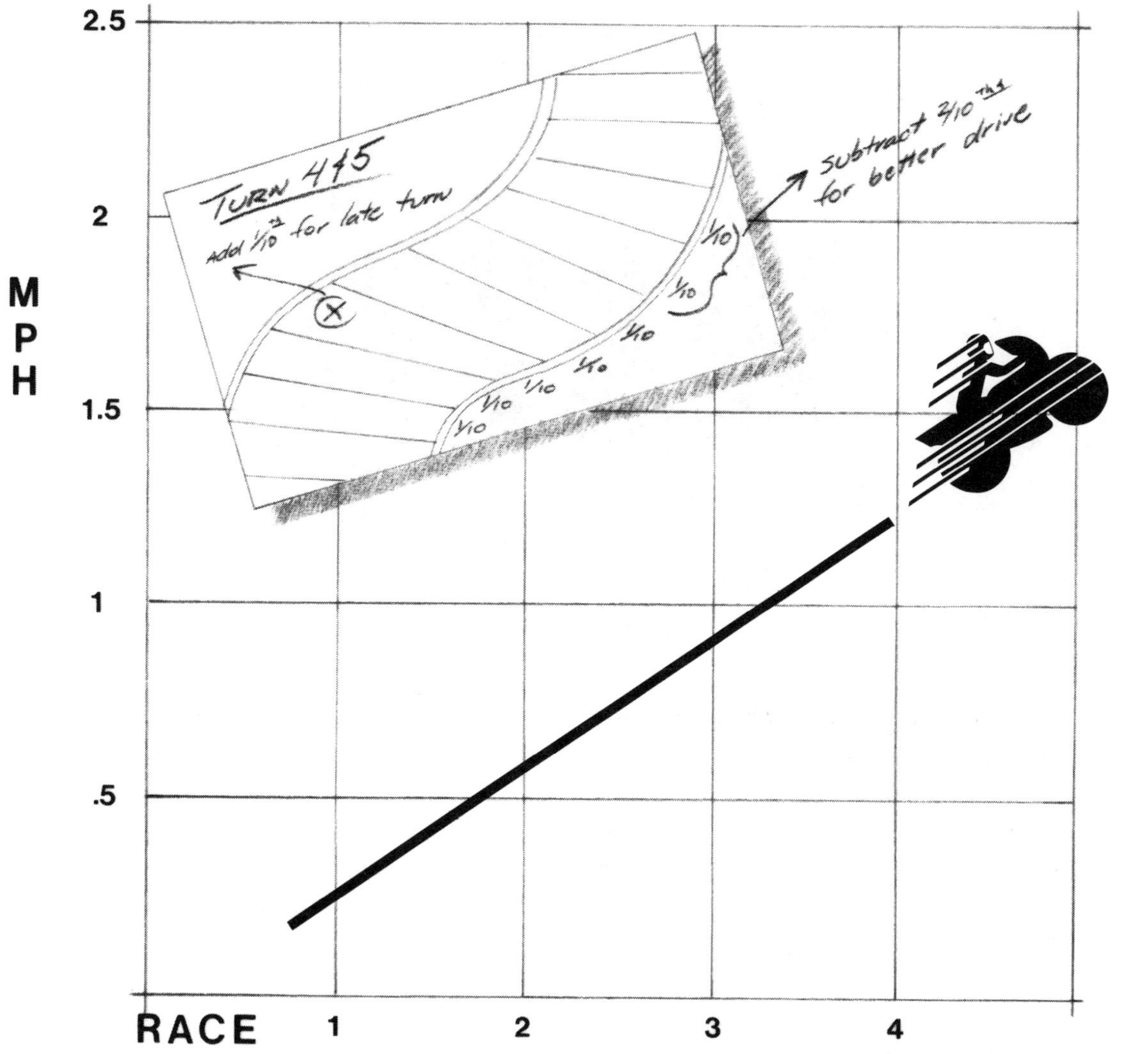
2.5
2
1.5
1
.5
M P H
RACE
1
2
3
4
TURN 4+5
add 1/10 for late turn
subtract 2/10ths for better drive

From another perspective, you are looking to improve each session about ¼ **mph** average speed around the track. That is not a lot of speed but it is enough to get your **target**. Going ¼ **mph** faster does not call for any major or dramatic changes in what you are doing, it requires small changes and not in one turn but all of them.

That is what this book is all about: Taking apart your riding and putting it back together, time after time, to find those ¼ seconds, 1/10th seconds or 1/100ths of a second, whatever you need to **win**.

Sometimes what you do seems slower but it's usually better not to overdo it. If you blow it in one section you will be slower in the next because you weren't able to think ahead.

Riding And Racing

Be forewarned, riding and racing motorcycles can become an addiction. Credit cards, friends and other pursuits have a way of becoming secondary to a real racing habit.

Racing is a high that is hard to beat. Time has a way of becoming suspended during intense racing. Heavy concentration and danger have the effect of making it "greater than life." Try not to alienate your family, your friends and the rest of life for the sake of racing. Don't burn yourself out.

Advice

Just one piece of advice.

Do not ask yourself any questions that start with the word "why"; they cannot be answered.

I'll tell you **why**.

I have found really excellent riders sitting in some vast problem about their riding and when I've asked them what it was, it always starts out with: "I can't understand **why** such and such a turn isn't going right," or "Why can't I go through here faster?" etc.

For a while I played a game. "Why isn't it going right?"

"I think I should be going faster."

"Why do you think you should be going faster?"

"Because guys are passing me there."

"Why are they passing you?"

"They are going faster."

"Why are they going faster?"

"They are on the gas harder."

"Why are they on the gas harder than you?"

"I'm afraid to go faster."

"Why are you afraid to go faster?"

This can go on forever without coming up with any answer, and that is a waste of time for you.

If you ask questions that begin with "what," "when," "how," "where," "which," "how many," "how much," etc., you get results.

The above example could then break down like this:

"What isn't going right?"

"My cornering speed isn't high enough."

"Which turn?"

"Number 3." (You get a specific)

"How can you tell you aren't going fast enough?"

"I'm getting passed." (Another specific.)

"Where are they passing you?"

"Going in." (You narrow it down even more.)

"What happens after that?"

"I catch everyone in the middle and on the exit."

"Is it really your cornering speed that is the problem?"

"Not really, but if I could go faster I could repass them on the exit."

"Can you go that much faster in the middle and exit?"

"I don't think I really can."

"Fine, how else can you handle it?"

"I could try braking even earlier and going underneath them on the way in because they go wide on the entrance or, #2, I could move over a little and make it harder for them to get set up on the brakes." (Now the rider has a simple plan to try, it may or may not work)

What Is A Plan?

Let's start out with the definition of a plan and let the rest of the book fill in the rest for you.

Your understanding and use of the 5 senses of racing:

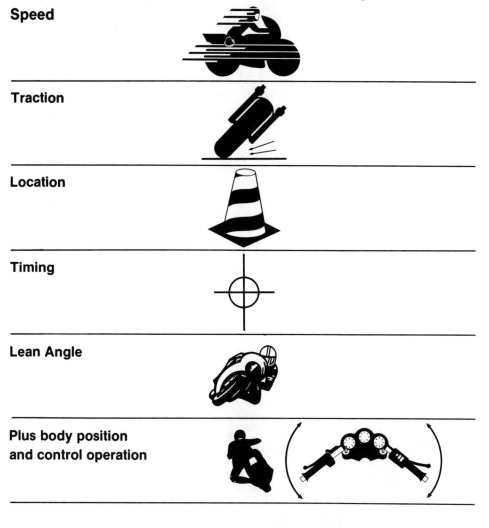

Speed

Traction

Location

Timing

Lean Angle

Plus body position and control operation

=Your Plan

Let's see if you can make some **plans** that will work.

CHAPTER I

How You Ride

It's The Thought That Counts

You really can change your ideas and go faster.

Riding a motorcycle can be broken down into two simple things: **Thought** and **motion**.

How you ride (motion) is determined by your ideas (thoughts) of how the riding should be done. When you come to a turn in the road, you size it up from your experience (motion you have experienced), you formulate an idea (thought) on how to take the turn this time (motion/thought), then you go through the turn (motion again). Your **idea** of how the turn should be ridden determines how well it all works out. You turned your **thoughts** and **ideas** into **motion**.

A lot of things could still be foggy while I'm working my times down but I try and ride "comfortable" even when I'm hangin it out.

Obviously, if your ideas match up with the road and the machine — how the bike works, the turn and its construction, your estimated speed, how much braking is required, how many gears to go down and so on — you'll probably do a good job with that turn. If your idea doesn't fit with the rest of these factors, you'll likely make mistakes, have a problem with some part of the turn, and find yourself doing things that seem somewhat out of your control.

The rider turns thoughts and ideas into motion.

Missing Link

A classic example of the missing link is the rider who comes out to the starting line armed with the **idea** of getting a good start. He knows the engine must be spinning fast enough to move the bike when he lets out the clutch, or the bike will bog on the line (idea). From watching other riders, he has borrowed another **idea**: turning the throttle on and off rapidly to keep the bike's revs up. But when the flag is dropped, the bike bogs at the start!

In this case, the rider's **idea** has a part missing. The missing part is that the throttle must be "on" when the clutch is let out. This rider let the clutch out when the throttle was in the off position! As a result, the rider unsuccessfully tried to turn his **thoughts into motion**. You might laugh, but I've seen this very situation occur time after time. It has happened to me when my own ideas matched the above scene: it is especially a problem with two-stroke machines in which the flywheel effect isn't great enough to keep the engine's momentum high for a good start. If you have ever experienced inconsistent starts, or know someone who complains about them, this probably is one of the causes. Has this ever happened to you?

When you first go out concentrate on the big things about the bike, transmission gears, tires and suspension.

Turn Motion Into Thought

In the pits, you turn motion into thoughts.

This is the flip side of the above situation. Most riders seem to have difficulty with this part, which is where learning takes place. Say you've gone around a turn, and it went pretty well but not perfectly. You run through the turn in your mind later to see if something can be changed for the better.

Note: If you're at a racetrack, I want you to realize that the time to think out your riding is "in the pits," you simply don't have enough time on the track, between corners, to do the kind of thinking that's necessary. You are **recording motion** as you ride so you'll have something to think about when you have the time. You change the motion that just occurred out on the track into **thoughts**, so that you can think about your riding. The best riders do some of this thinking out on the track, while riding, and can make it work. Most of us should beware of changes, especially big ones, while we're riding.

What you do is freshest after the first 5 minutes of practice. That's the time you should think it out. Get your bike figured out and then your riding. Come in and tell your mechanic what is going on, let him get started and then go think it over.

Mind Movie

If you've ever tried to examine your riding by looking at your own mind "movie" of what happened on the track or the road, you probably found it isn't easy. Things can become confused, and parts of the track seem to be missing. Often, you can't remember just what you were doing in a turn. You might have a vague recollection of accelerating out of a turn, but it's hard to get the exact feeling. You know you were looking at something while going into the turn, but you can't remember what it was. This imprecise recollection happens to everyone, to some degree.

Just as a movie has both an audio track and a video track, your own mental recording of what happened has two tracks: **thoughts** and **motion**. Trying to deal with both tracks at once can cause problems. If you're in the pits trying to get the "feel" of the acceleration coming off a turn, but while riding you paid attention to where you were going (looking ahead so as not to run off the track), the precise feeling of the **motion** will not be in your "movie." You don't have it because you weren't recording it.

The same thing holds true for the rider with the bad start. He was probably watching the starter's flag. When he tried to think over what he did to get such a bad start, the information isn't there, because he wasn't paying enough **attention** to the throttle and clutch. If you've ever tried and failed to get a fast start, try to remember just how you turn the throttle and let out the clutch at the start. Can you remember exactly how you do it?

Accurate recordings of what happened will give you much needed information.

The Rider Translates

It's hard to give advice because what would help my riding is not the same as someone else.

For a rider to change **thought** into **motion** and **motion** into **thought**, he's got to understand the **languages** of thought and motion. Riders who have done well at racing or even street riding have developed their own ways of thinking about the things that happen to them and to their machines. You must be able to do that as well. You must be able to translate what happens (motion) into thoughts, then translate those thoughts back into motion. That is the only way to improve on the racetrack. Does this make sense?

Italian Rider/Chinese Mechanic

Take this idea into another area. You come into the pits and your mechanic asks, "How's the bike working?" You say, "Well, you better fix this thing; it's junk." Your poor wrench tries again: "What's it doing?" You say, "I don't know, I just can't ride it." Your chances of getting a factory ride would be poor to nonexistent if you supplied that kind of information. The rider in this scene can't **translate motion into thought**.

And the rider then leaves the mechanic in the same position. The mechanic doesn't have enough information about what the bike is doing (motion) to come up with any ideas (thought) on how to fix it. The rider is speaking the wrong language.

Test Yourself

As a rider, you must repeatedly ask yourself questions in order to improve. For example: Your competition continues to pass you in Turn 3, and it really bothers you. You come into the pits and you think about Turn 3. What are you doing in that section? If your only answer is, "I don't want to be passed there," you aren't going to get very far. On the other hand, if your answer is, "When I take that low line (motion) going into the turn, I always have to back off the throttle or I'll run off the track, and that's exactly where I'm being passed," you can help yourself. You have something to work with. **You've translated motion into thought**. You already do this to some extent.

Step 2 involves translating the thought back into motion. You say to yourself, "OK, I'm running wide and losing my drive off Turn 3. I'll have to find a new place to turn into it, so I can get the drive." You think it out further, "If I wait until that next patch of pavement to turn, 10 feet further down the track, I'll be able to get a later apex and a better drive." Now you are turning your thoughts into a **plan** that will change your motion. You translated it! If the plan works on the track and your times improve, you have translated the thought correctly into motion.

Under Test Yourself. Drawing pictures on paper is really good for figuring out what you're doing. You can see WHAT and WHERE, when you make the drawing.

Translation Problems

On paper, the above example works out nicely. It's very simple, and often something just that simple can be done. More often, however, riding problems take finer adjustments by the rider than just turning 10 feet later into a turn.

If you're distracted by something, the above **plan** won't work. A rider has to know what is important when he tries to make a change for the better. In the example of trying to go in "deep" to get a better drive, if by changing the braking the rider locked up the front wheel just before he was going to turn, he's probably missed his new turning point. What is sure is that he should have been looking at his new plan to turn, right at that point, and instead he had to pay **attention** to the sliding wheel.

In this case, the rider was unable to turn the thought into motion because he was distracted. When he translated his thoughts into a plan,

You've really got to work to move a turn entry marker up deeper.

9

he forgot to take into account that it wouldn't work if he was trying to brake hard and turn at the same time. This is a **translation** problem. He forgot that you can't say "turn hard and brake hard" in the language of motorcycle motion. It won't work.

In this workbook, we will sort out the language of **motion** and of **thought** into tidy packages that you can use to improve your riding. **Think of it as improving your ability to translate motion and thought.**

You Ride An Idea

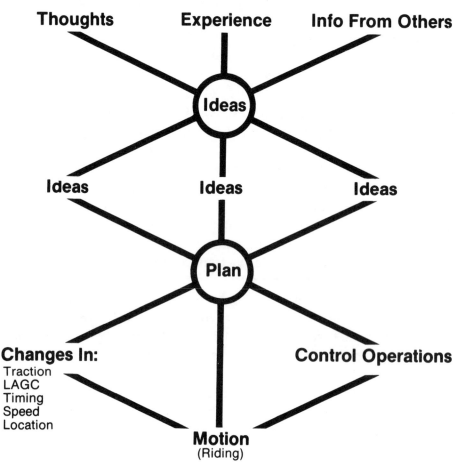

Out on the track, your thoughts — and the ideas that have come from those thoughts — will determine how you get around the track. Your ideas, combined with the ideas of others that you have learned from, will — and do — make up your **plan** at each of the hundreds of places that call for planning. It could be said that you **ride an idea**, not the bike or the track. The idea you come up with is the result of your thoughts. Your plan is the result of those ideas and how you translate them into motion.

The fact that each rider's idea is slightly different becomes obvious when you watch film of the top riders in the world going around the same turn. Each rider clearly has a different idea, because each rides distinctly different lines. Each of them sees the turn in a different way. Each has a different idea of how to do it. The additional fact that often those riders' times vary by only hundredths of a second is further proof that any basically good plan will work, "if" the rider has taken the time to think it out (thought) and put it to work (motion).

Plan Test

Imagine yourself behind the bubble of Eddie Lawson's or Freddie Spencer's bike in a 150-mile turn, sliding the tires, rolling the gas on and feeling confident that you'll get around the turn in one piece. Go ahead and try. It should be obvious that their **ideas** of what is happening on the track are very accurate. They have to be. Their plans are well worked out. Their thoughts are accurately translated into motion. The motion they experienced was accurately translated into thoughts.

Limits

Improvement has no limits; someone always comes along who is a little bit faster. A rider who is faster than you has a better grasp of how to **translate thoughts into motion**. With a better understanding of your own language of thought and motion, you will be a better rider.

A good example of this principle is the rider whose bike is geared improperly. The rider knows he's having trouble in two or three turns of the infield. He wants to get a better drive off those turns, and he really feels he should be able to do it. The gearing problem puts him into those turns at the redline of the machine, and he has to shift while the bike is leaned over almost all the way. The upshift must be made carefully, or the bike probably will slide when he gets back on the gas. The drive suffers from this gear change. It isn't smooth, and he loses time.

If this rider can't figure out what is wrong, he'll be limited forever on those turns, because he can't translate **motions** on the track into a clear **thought**, produce an **idea**, then change his bike or his riding to correct the problem.

Look over any part of your riding that you can, and see if it doesn't fall into either **thought** or **motion**.

You can't do 110% all the time. It's not fun to ride on the edge, getting away with sliding and so on. It's OK but then once you get used to kickin the back end out in some turn and it's comfortable, you then don't know what will happen if you go past that.

A guy who is going a few seconds a lap slower than me has got to go over this stuff. He has to. I've made up my mind on lots of it in 16 years of racing. He hasn't, so he will have to do the mechanical learning just like I did.

Top riders have thought it through many times. They make it look easy.

11

Chapter Recap

1. Riding can be divided into **thoughts** and **motion**.
2. How you ride is determined by your **ideas**.
3. As a rider, you **translate** your ideas into different motions of riding.
4. If your idea of how to do something doesn't match the realities of your bike or the track, you do it wrong. If your idea is right, you have a good chance of doing it right.
5. An idea with a part missing will produce poor results on the track.
6. You **translate** the things that happen to you out on the track (motion) into thoughts about riding.
7. You take those thoughts and examine them, decide to change something, then turn your new thoughts into a **plan** to do something different on the track.
8. Making new plans while riding can be dangerous because they haven't been thought out.
9. Looking over your riding can be difficult. If your **attention** was being spent on the motion of the bike, you probably weren't paying much attention to the **plan** or **idea**. If you were thinking about what you "should" be doing (your plan), you probably didn't have much attention on the motion or how well the plan worked.
10. A rider is limited by how well he can **translate** his motion on the track into thought, and then turn his thought back into motion.
11. You ride by your **idea** of how to ride, and each rider has a different idea of how to do each thing.

Questions And Drills

1. Pick a turn that you know well.
2. Play back your own "mental movie" of it.
3. Try to recall the thoughts you have about it.
4. What are the thoughts you have while "riding" it? (Write them down.)
5. What motion do you experience in it?

If you have trouble recalling those thoughts:

1. Go back over the things you looked at while you were on the track.
2. What did they mean to you?

    For example: If you have some **reference point in a turn**:
    a) What does it mean to you if the bike is at one side or the other of it?
    b) Does it mean you are running wide?
    c) Does it mean you can let the bike swing out further?
    d) Does it mean you can get on the gas?

Those are all thoughts about motion.

1. Do you have any thoughts like these?
2. Do you think of things like this while riding?
3. Do you think of things like this after riding?
4. Does this whole process of thinking things through seem useless?
5. Could you handle it easier by just riding?
6. Can your riding improve?
    a) By spending more time on thought?
    b) By spending more time on riding?

CHAPTER II

The Soft Science

Your Senses And Science. Where Do They Meet?

There are a lot of little things you think about, it's like having alot of little brains hooked up to one central brain. I think about alot of things at once.

It's every bit as hard to describe racing as it is to define the changing colors of a sunset. Quadrillions of dust particles float in the air, reflecting the sun as it ever so slowly drops out of sight. Each of those particles differs from each other, each shifting and turning in the setting sun's exotic light. You look on in wonder, awe. . . .

Kenny, Freddie, Eddie and Wayne come around a series of turns, all racing on the same track, and all turning the same controls, all bound to earth by the laws of physics, all running within hundredths of seconds of one another, and each doing it "differently." You look on in wonder, awe.

There are four guys out there doing the same thing just about as differently as it can be done, and there's just no way to break the action down exclusively into a hard science. Don't get me wrong, racing is not just a seat-of-the-pants activity. It's basically analytical, but describing it is just as hard as describing a sunset. You see one part of it; I see another. Kenny, Randy and the rest see one track; you see quite another. Each sees his own track.

Motion, Feelings And Senses

You experience **motion** through your **senses**. You have senses such as sight and touch, hearing, smell, balance, depth perception and many more. Each of these can be divided into smaller subdivisions. Sight, for instance, includes contrast, color, shades of color, focus and still more. Each sense is slightly different from one person to another. These abilities combine, allowing you to judge speed, angle, braking force, cornering forces and the other motions of riding. You **sense** these things. They are your input.

Spend more attention on the things that are hard. Put it on what you want to change.

From past experience, good or bad, you have **feelings** about some kinds of motion. You like a certain speed — producing a good feeling — or you don't; yielding a bad uneasy sensation. You might like tight turns, but not if they're bumpy. Perhaps high-speed turns really excite you, or

Each rider has different
thoughts and feelings
about every turn.

they might make you feel apprehensive. You can lean your bike over
only so far; you have your limit.

When you enter a turn, all the experience you have with similar turns
comes into play. You judge the turn with the best knowledge you have
on hand. While you are riding, that knowledge and experience might
take the form of **feelings** about what happens to you. Different kinds of
motion can have feelings which generate different **thoughts**.

Say you enter a turn and it **feels** too fast. So, you roll off the throttle a
little, maybe. Or you get into a certain lean angle and find it's uncomfortable to go any further. Or you roll on the gas and **sense** the acceleration
coming out of a turn; a certain amount is just right and anything else is
either too fast or too slow.

**You sense the motion, and each different kind of motion can produce
different feelings/thoughts.**

*When I come into a turn I
know I'm going to steer it
within a few inches of
where I did last time but I
can set it up so fast it
almost seems "automatic".*

Sampling

Sampling is the process through which you measure what is happening against your idea of what is "supposed" to happen. For example: You are ready to take a shower. You turn on the hot water, let it run until it seems to be at maximum heat, then you start to add cold water to bring the mix to the "right" temperature.

You put your hand into the water to **sample** the temperature. You check that temperature against your **idea** of what that temperature should be. After an adjustment, you check the water again against your **idea** of the "right" temperature. That is **sampling; measuring what you sense against what your idea says it is supposed to be**.

Sampling is matching idea with your senses. You do it all the time.

Racing Samples

Nothing's really automatic it's just that some of the learning barely takes me any time to do it. I've been through it so many times, I don't have to do it in the mechanical way anymore.

You start with an **idea** of how fast you can go or how far you can lean your bike over. The idea came from thoughts you had about motion. The **input of sensation** you get while doing the riding is judged against your idea of how things should be or what they should feel like. **Too fast, for you, is faster than your idea of how fast to go.**

Your **translation** (of the thoughts and motion that are going on) has ideas attached to it: Something is good, or not so good; some action will work or it won't work; something scares you; or it doesn't. Whatever you sense and feel while you are riding is the constant back and forth a rider goes through of **judging** his thoughts against the motion that is occurring.

You are **sampling the motion**, putting that sensation up to your idea of how it should be, **sampling your idea**, then your attention goes back on the motion and so on. **Sampling is done by switching your attention back and forth from motion to thought, then from thought back to motion**.

Have you ever gone through a turn while changing the throttle position to try to find the right speed? The process involves your back and forth sampling of the speed against your idea of what speed it should be, along with the other factors you notice, lean angle, tire adhesion, line, reference points, pavement condition and many more. Sampling is the most basic of rider activities.

In racing, sampling is a precision skill.

Feelings: Good Or Bad

Having **feelings** is also a basic rider activity, but feelings can be a problem. An example of a problem with feelings is the old riding myth that you'd flip over forward if you used the front brake. Any rider who was taught this way has a very bad feeling about using the front brake!

The **thought** was planted there by someone, and the **motion** of using the front brake now seems very dangerous to the rider who allowed that thought to grow. The result was a feeling; a **thought** becomes attached to a **motion**.

If I am confused about something like where to brake, I might brake really deep and blow the turn on purpose.

The bad part about having feelings toward things that happen while riding is that you don't allow yourself to go through the process of **sampling**, especially if the feelings are negative ones. For instance, most riders will not take kindly to sand on the road if they've ever fallen in it. Completely avoiding the sand is their best way to handle the situation. Logically, however, if you fell in sand or dirt on the road, the best choice would be to learn how to handle it. When a rider avoids a situation associated with bad feelings, he'll never learn anything more about it, because he isn't willing to experience it again. He isn't willing to sample.

Physics

Physics is a method of describing the interaction of matter and energy. It isn't an attempt to describe any **thoughts** you might have about this interaction.

Your **ideas** and **feelings** about going around a turn, at least to begin with, wouldn't be affected by what a tire engineer tells you about how sticky his tires are. Physics is a "hard science" dealing with particles; riding is a "soft science," which deals with how you **feel** about what you are doing while you ride.

Even though a scientist can tell you what is going on while you ride, in terms of mass, inertia, coefficients of friction, gyroscopic effect, center of gravity and much more, he'll never be able to explain why two riders on identical bikes don't go around the track at the same speed, or why they both turn the same lap times when one rider is faster in one section of the track and the other is faster in a different place!

It's clear that physics deals with half of our basic ingredients: **thought** and **motion**. Physics, however, is the wrong language to describe **motion** — at least, from a rider's point of view. Physics doesn't handle the interplay between thought and motion, and that is where you put your **attention**. That is how you ride.

Physics Rider

I once had a rider come to my Superbike School at Laguna Seca, and he crashed toward the end of the day. When we questioned him about what had happened, he told us, "I can't figure it out. I'm an engineering student, and my mother is an engineer, we're both heavy into physics. We sat down and figured this whole thing out by the physics of what happens while riding, and there was no way I could crash."

Obviously, there was a flaw in his calculations. They didn't account for **sampling**. This is another example of how **a thought or idea can determine what a rider does on the track**.

You can't always do it because someone says you can.

"Let's see; E = MC² offset by the coefficient of friction my leathers have over a 1.736 sq. ft. area = Road Rash!"

Physics Language

The language of physics is much too cumbersome to be employed by a rider while he is riding, but it has its place and importance. For instance, it is helpful to know that in banked turns the force of gravity pulls the bike and rider toward the inside of the turn. It's good to know, but it isn't necessary to know it.

Your ability to **sense** what is happening in a turn, along with your ideas, is invariably of more concern than the physical laws governing your riding. If you are one second faster from one practice to the next, you can bet that the physics involved didn't change much, but your **ideas** and **feelings** on what you were doing "did" change — for the better.

I set up the bike to feel good in the important turns, usually the fast ones. It might feel bad or even be dangerous in others.

Managing Thought And Motion

Riding is a soft science, because it involves how the rider **feels** about what he is doing. That feeling **can't** be put into an equation or law, and it can't be diagramed or mapped out with mathematics. How you think and sense motion are governed by one more factor: **attention**.

You spend attention on each thing you do. Spend it wisely.

Attention

You spend attention on everything you do. And you don't have an unlimited supply of it. Consider your attention like a fixed sum of money: If you have $10 in your pocket, and you spend $5, you have just $5 left. If you spend the full $10, you have no money left. Your attention is the same. If you spend all of it on one thing, you can't spend any of it on another. In a turn, you might spend your entire $10 worth of attention on **sampling** what you're doing. On the straightaway, you probably spend a lot less. You can look at your pit board and relax on the straight. Now, imagine what would happen if you had to read pit signals in a turn. You wouldn't have enough attention left over to make sense out of the signals without slowing down.

Everything you do with your motorcycle costs some part of your $10 worth of attention. You've probably noticed that when you brake hard, most of your attention is on the brake force. You are spending a lot sampling what's happening there. You couldn't look over your shoulder to see if another rider was closing in while you were braking hard, because you just wouldn't have the attention to spare for that. At that point, you're effectively broke, and you can't afford to buy that look over your shoulder.

Sampling And Attention

As you ride, you spend some part of your **attention** on **thought** and some part on **motion**. You monitor the motion with your senses, see if your idea of how the motion should be matches up with how the motion really is, then go back to sensing motion again. **Sampling is the keystone thought process of riding**.

You pay, in the currency of attention, a price for each thing you sense. You pay for each time you check your **ideas** and **plans** for a given action, and for **everything** else that you allow yourself to notice or consider. As you spend your attention on one thing, your ability to spend it on other things is decreased.

What's It Worth?

How much of your **attention** you spend on each factor of your riding depends on how important each is to what you are doing. For instance, it is generally unimportant to spend attention on tire traction while you are on the straightaway. When you're in a turn, however, traction is very important and should be bought. Riders generally pay a lot of attention to cornering clearance, especially on production bikes.

Likewise, where you're going in the turn costs a lot. And sensing your speed might cost more than anything else. All of these things, in fact, cost something each time you ride a turn, and when you ride it well, you spend the right amount on each of them.

Good Investments

To get the most of your $10 worth of attention, you have to spend it wisely. If you spend too much on just sensing motion, and none on your plans and ideas, you'll likely become lost on the track. This happens commonly after an unexpected slide. All of the rider's attention immediately goes to stability and traction. While he's concentrating on traction, he quits paying for the rest of the important things for that moment, and so becomes a little lost. The slide didn't take up much time, but getting his attention back on the job did.

Spending too much time on your **plan of action** will produce the same sort of results as the traction example, though in a different way. You quit spending attention on **feedback** from the machine, and your ability to sense speed, traction and everything else goes down — as your lap times increase. If you want to concentrate on one particular problem or technique, that's OK; then you aren't concerned with lap times, and you simply set a speed that won't cost a lot of attention to maintain.

If you can't remember what you are doing at some part of the track, your attention is stuck on motion. Not enough is being spent on thought.

So the best investment with your attention is to spend a little bit on both sensing motion and monitoring your plan. The amount of both investments might seem about equal, but they're not. **The plan, which came from your thoughts and ideas, is, without a doubt, the most important part.** Without a plan, most of the information you get from your senses is wasted. You have no way to measure it.

TURN #1				STRAIGHT

An investment chart of attention can be made for any track situation.

1. Traction
2. Speed
3. Timing
4. Lean Angle
5. Location

Entry

1	2	3	4	5
$2	$2	$4	$1	$1

Middle

1	2	3	4	5
$3	$2	$1	$1	$2

Exit

1	2	3	4	5
$3	$1	$1	$2	$2

1. 0

2. 0

3. $.50

4. 0

5. $2.00

21

Plan Ahead

Your senses don't "see" into the next moment, your plan does. Your plan sets the stage so you can tell yourself how everything should feel at a given moment. For example, a decreasing-radius turn. If you don't have a plan to handle that kind of corner, you will always find yourself going into it too fast, because your senses tell you it's OK to be going that fast at the entrance or even the middle of the turn. At the exit, you'll run too far out, and you'll have to roll back the throttle. Once you learn that decreasing-radius turns won't allow you to enter the turn hot, you can adjust your speed and line so that you don't run out of track. Without a plan, there is no way for you to ever get it right.

The nice thing about a plan is that you can make it in the pits and just use it on the track. If you haven't concocted a plan of one kind or another, you are always riding at the limit, which can become tiring. You're still having fun, you just become tired quicker.

You've got to have it planned before you do it, you've got to!

With your plan set, you can spend most of your attention on sensing the changing motion, and a lot less on where you're going and what you want to do. You can start to control your machine, because you know in advance what you want it to do.

How It Works For You

You use this information to look over your riding to discover where you are spending your **attention** on thought and motion. You look to see where you are switching attention back and forth with the **sampling** procedure. Only then can you begin to **decide** where you want to spend it.

I think the guys coming up need to do these steps.

Chapter Recap

1. You experience **motion** through your **senses**. All of the forces and sensations — both good and bad — of riding are part of your riding.
2. **Feelings** often become associated with different kinds of motion while riding.
3. **Sampling** is the process of sensing motion and measuring it against the **idea** of how it is supposed to be going. Your idea of how fast, how much lean angle and so on, is contained in your thoughts, plan and ideas about riding. Sampling is how you judge your progress.
4. The process of sampling costs **attention**. You spend your attention on motion, to see how things are going. You then switch attention to the thought or idea you have about how it should be done. You make a decision based on those two things. If you decide things aren't going as they should, you can change that aspect of your riding.
5. Having certain **feelings** about riding can stop or slow your improvement. Negative feelings can keep you from investigating and handling a riding problem.
6. The laws of physics and the language of science do not look at rid-

ing the same way a rider does.

7. The rider must decide what is important, and then spend his attention on his thoughts or on motion, depending on what is happening and where he is on the track. Having a **plan** really means that the rider has decided what is important, and has planned where to spend his attention.

Questions And Drills

1. What is the worst thing that ever happened to you on a motorcycle?
2. What is the best thing?
3. List the things that make you feel bad while riding.
4. List the things that make you feel good.
5. What other things about riding have feelings connected to them?
6. Are you "blind" in those areas that have feelings connected to them?
7. How well do you judge speed?
8. How well do you judge lean angle?
9. How well do you judge tire traction?
10. How well do you judge braking forces?
11. Do you ever become lost on the track?
12. What kinds of turns do you do worst?
13. What kinds of turns do you do best?
14. List the places on the track where you are tense.
   a) Where is your attention being spent at those places?
   b) Is it being spent on **thoughts** or on **motion**?
   c) Is what you are spending it on important?
   d) Where should you be spending it?
   e) How is your **control** of the bike at these places?
15. Pick a turn you handle well.
   a) Do you have a **plan**?
   b) Does your plan include where you should spend your **attention**?
16. Talk with someone about a turn you have both ridden.
   a) Find out how the other rider spends his attention.
   b) Are the things he thinks about the same as yours?
   c) Are they different?
17. Think of a turn you know you are spending your attention on in the wrong place.
   a) Make a plan to spend your attention carefully.
   b) What is different about this new plan?
   c) Decide whether you can do it or not.

When doing the questions you will find the parts where you are tense.

CHAPTER III

Thought

Is That A Thought, Idea or Plan?

Unlike **motion**, which can be observed and categorized with a vast storehouse of scientific terms, **thought** has remained a mysterious process, and very little of it has been observed in its raw form. For instance, it is easy to observe a ball rolling downhill, gather speed, then run into an object with some amount of force. The scientist can then go on to determine how much force is generated at what speeds, and formulate mathematical equations from that observation, which can be used to design any number of machines. He can measure the ball's weight with a scale. He can time the ball's motion, and can measure the force with which it hit. In short, all of the tools he needs are readily available to him.

It's hard to change your mind about a line, you can get stuck.

Thought is more difficult to observe, mostly because there is very little, or no, observable motion to it. You can't tell what kind of thought is going on by looking at someone, and often, the person himself does not feel totally in control of the thought process. Thoughts happen rapidly, and are subject to change without notice. Thoughts sometimes have **feelings** attached to them, which can cloud up an issue. Very few tools have been designed to handle thought, and little exists for you to help work with them. If such an implement as a **thought vice** existed, you could hold onto your thoughts, reshaping them as you can metal objects, but there's no such thing. Few agree on what **thought** really is.

The rider who can plan his actions from his thoughts, is in control.

The Soft Science

Because **thought** is elusive and can change so easily from one thing to another and because **thought** directs motion, roadracing is a Soft Science.

We try to match what we see and sense to what we cannot see. The point at which thought and motion meet and interact is where a rider learns how to cut his lap times — or where he never will. For example: You ride into a turn with the **idea** of how fast you want to be going. You can't see that idea, but you can sense and adjust your speed. You take real motion and try to align it with your thoughts about motion. If your thoughts are close to the bike's actual motion, you're right. If they don't match, you're wrong.

Thoughts out on the track don't work out sometimes if you want to change something. You have to fit it in with the rest of the pieces of the puzzle.

Scale Of Control

1. When your thoughts about motion match the real motion, you are right.
2. When you can consistently match the motion with your thoughts, you are a good rider.
3. When you can think through a turn and **plan** the motion, you are a very good rider.
4. When you can plan and **predict** motion — and the changes in motion — and can adjust them while riding to suit your plan, you are the best.

Race Think

For a racer, the whole business of **thought** can be broken into bite-size chunks: All you are really interested in is getting the riding job done, which allows you to gauge your thoughts against an absolute scale like the above. You can ask:
1. Did an action work or didn't it?
2. Did the lap times come down?
3. Did it make the riding easier?
4. Did what happened on the track match your **idea** of what was going to happen?
5. Did your **plan** improve your riding?
6. Did your **plan** match the way the turn really was?

The Steps To Plan

As you ride, you record your impressions of the track and everything that you notice. What you don't notice, you don't record. The things you record are determined by where you had your **attention** while you were riding. You didn't notice any dirt on the outside of Turn 7, because you weren't riding on the outside of it, so the dirt wasn't important to you. You "did" notice that someone had changed the position of a marker cone from the first practice to the second. You also noticed some bumps on the inside of Turn 4. You went to the outside of a pavement patch in another turn. It seemed unwise to turn on the throttle at a place you thought you could. These impressions of what you noticed could go on and on.

When you notice something about riding, it becomes a thought about riding.

That is the first step, to go out on a track and notice things. Those things you see and feel turn into **thoughts**. The second step involves **ideas**. When you combine thoughts with what you already understand about riding, the thoughts become ideas about riding. For example: Noticing that the bike will run outside in Turn 2 if you give it a certain amount of throttle means nothing until you get the **idea** to change the throttle position so the bike won't run wide. And what you noticed about Turn 2 would continue to mean nothing without the vital process that takes place in between having a thought and coming up with an idea. That process is **translation**.

Translation

A lot of times when I change something like track position, I'm real uncomfortable and I have to do it until it works. You have to work into it.

A thought turns into an idea when you add experience and understanding. In a turn, the thought that you're running wide means nothing until you decide what it means. If running wide to you means "running off the track," you apply that meaning to it, and probably roll off the throttle. If running wide in a particular turn means to you that you should watch for your edge-of-the-track reference point and adjust the throttle, then you put that **idea into motion**. In either case, nothing happened until you compared the thought to your understanding (ideas you already have), and then turned it into the motion you believed was correct.

Procedure

Your thoughts translate into ideas, then arrive at the third stage, the **plan**. A plan is the result of putting an idea or ideas together to form a procedure, or, what you are going to do. Your procedure tells you how you're going to control your bike — and "how much" you are going to control it — to accomplish your plan.

In the turn where you've been running wide, you'll try to find a better reference point in the middle of the turn to let you know where the bike is, and how much throttle you can use. The alternative is to wait until you're into the turn far enough — and fast enough — to scare you.

You will have solved the immediate problem with the turn if this small plan fits into your overall plan. It might not, for instance, if your overall plan called for less speed on the exit because you had to set up for the next turn right away, and being at the outside of the track while carrying more speed makes it harder to turn.

The Decision

Coming up with a plan isn't really the final stage. There's one more step — to make the **decision** to act on the plan. You assemble some thoughts into ideas about the track and your riding. You turn these ideas into a plan of action with all the steps figured out. Finally, you **decide** to take the steps you've planned.

Making the decision isn't anything fancy, and it's not psyching up or out. It's just buckling down and doing what you've planned. Everyone has trouble putting good ideas into motion for lack of a firm **decision to act**. You just get lazy and don't do it. The same holds true for racing. You have to really push yourself to break old habits. It's not easy to change old plans, especially if they once worked. You have to make the decision to change and improve or someone will come along riding one second faster and make the decision for you!

Everytime I get on the bike I'm pumped because that's all I want to do.

Learning To Ride

Learning to be an excellent roadracer is a lot like the first ride you ever took on a motorcycle. Your friend tells you to "give it some gas and let out the clutch." This friend is providing two **ideas**, and you're supposed to make a **plan** out of it. Eventually, you combined the two ideas into a plan. But you didn't get it right the first time, did you?

Now, you are out at the track trying to get fast, and you have some ideas on how to do it. It's the same thing as learning to ride all over again. Don't make the mistake of believing you can race just because you can ride. That first day of riding, you were trying to turn the **ideas** of how to work the clutch into **motion**. Your overall plan wasn't much more involved than to get moving on the bike. But racing is a lot more complex than that first wobbly ride around the block. "Go out and race" is not much of a plan. It's a long way off from: "If I can turn the bike a little later, I can pick up 1/10th second."

I felt like I was really going fast when I first started racing. It doesn't seem like I changed that much.

Ability

There is something I've observed that is common to all very good and great riders. They all have the ability to reduce both the track and what they are doing on it into very small pieces.

For the new rider, there is not much more than "the track." He comes out to learn a racecourse, "to get some track time." After a while, he mentally breaks the track down into separate turns and sections. Next, he tries to work out parts of turns: The Entry, the Middle and the Exit of each turn. That's progress certainly, but unfortunately, that's just about as far as many riders ever get. Their thoughts, ideas and plans dead end at that point. Is your riding dead ended here too?

The Puzzle

Trying to put the puzzle together is hard. Some turns you think you can go harder but they are slick or off camber. Finally you should just realize it can't be done and concentrate on the drive instead of high corner speed or going in deeper.

When a plan is missing parts, or it suffers from one of the other things that can go wrong with any plan, you're just marking time on the track waiting for something to happen. Other riders who have figured things out are already acting on their plans, and are either passing or gaining on you. **A turn is like a puzzle**. Knowing what the picture looks like helps, but you still have to figure out where all of the individual parts fit.

Confining your thinking to the **entrance, middle** and **exit** of a turn is like knowing that each piece of the puzzle with a flat side belongs somewhere on the border of the picture. It isn't enough. The missing parts are where and how you are going to steer and change the speed of the bike.

So, you need to group the remaining parts. All of the green ones will be the trees and the grass. The grey will be the road surface. On the racetrack is when you would be figuring out the main things that have to be done, and where they fit into the overall turn. For example: In a long turn that has a couple of radius changes and that requires a slower speed at the Exit than in the Middle, you know that some speed will have to be scrubbed off somewhere in the turn. You narrow it down as you ride and change your plan. You find you can start to scrub the speed toward the end of the Middle rather than at the beginning of it.

After your practice is over, you come back in to think things out. You noticed that you were waiting for your final turning point, just coasting awhile before you got to it. That **thought** brings about the **idea** that you could move up your shut-off point. That idea might work, but it would be better still to fill in one more piece of the puzzle first. Find a new place to shut off, so the new part of the **plan** has something to hook onto. You don't want to be holding onto that old idea of where to shut off while you're trying to work in a new one at the same time.

To change the place where you do something on a track, you must first locate the place, then signal yourself that it is time to act.

Each turn is a puzzle. Where do the parts go. Entry, exit, roll on, hard drive, slide, etc.

Thoughts And Motion Revisited

All of your thoughts, ideas, plans, decisions, samplings, feelings and actions deal with speed changes and steering. All of those thoughts, ideas, etc. are limited by traction and they should be part of your overall plan. **Each costs attention.**

Organize Your Thoughts

A plan to do something on a racetrack is much the same as any other plan you have from day to day. Say, for example, that Betty Sue looks pretty good to you; when you look at her, **thoughts** happen. Perhaps an **idea** comes from those thoughts to ask her out for a date. You begin to form a **plan** on how to ask her out, and where you'll take her.

The process is much the same for riding. You ride around a racetrack or down a piece of road, looking at what there is to see. You have thoughts about what you see. Some turns are easy, some hard, some are familiar, some new to you. In the places on the track that you understand, ideas on how to ride come easily, and perhaps a plan occurs to you right away. Turn 9 is really similar to Turn 6 at another track, and you apply the plan you developed for that one to this.

You apply your thoughts and ideas to the track and come up with a plan.

A Plan Is Action

A plan, even a good one, is no guarantee of success; any plan is only as good as its execution. What you actually do with it determines the outcome of the plan. A good plan, carried out well, produces a good result.

You have to really try your new plan. If you don't, you never get to the next step or the newer plan.

So, back to your plan to date Betty Sue. You close in on her to ask her for a date, and you've decided on the Bold Approach: "Hey, honey, wanna go out on Friday night?" She looks at you like you're nuts, and continues talking to her friend. Your execution might have been perfect, but it was a bad plan to start with. And, as you found out in this case, a bad plan produces a bad result.

You decide that turn #6 can be exited wide open because it looks like turn #9 and that one is wide open. That's your plan and it's the **bold** approach. The rough pavement on the exit gets you sideways and off the track when you try it. Bad plan.

It probably would have helped to have asked Betty Sue her name first. In the same way, it probably would have been good to have checked out the pavement on the outside of Turn 6. Both of these plans were missing essential parts which made them unworkable. They both went to the plan-of-action stage without enough thought.

Planned Problems

Plans can easily produce more problems than any that they might solve. Your plan can create problems, like the one above, if it falls short of handling the real situation the track presents. There are several potential shortcomings of any plan.

A plan with missing parts creates unknown results.

1. **Missing parts**. A plan that is missing parts puts the rider in a holding pattern while he waits for something to happen. No action has been planned, so nothing happens. In a turn, you feel indecisive where the parts are missing from the plan. Usually, you'll roll the throttle off in these areas even though there wasn't any good reason for you to slow up.

I try to keep everything the same with my riding when testing so I can feel out the equipment.

It is easier to notice a plan that is missing parts in a long sweeper, because the indecision that results from missing parts takes up more track, it lasts longer. In shorter turns, the indecision is just as critical, but the results of the indecision are more immediate. Example: Not having a precise turning point when entering a turn will force the rider to put his **attention** on the steering, to see if it worked out. While his attention is focused on steering, he misses his mid-turn **reference points**, and blows the rest of the turn.

Where your plan is missing parts, your attention is on the motion, but there's no idea to tell you whether the motion is right or not. Sampling is haphazard in these parts, and you feel unsure of yourself.

Good thoughts but not a plan yet.

1. COME ON OUTSIDE OF #2
2. NOT GOING FAST ENOUGH IN MIDDLE
3. BRAKING TOO HARD
4. ENTERING ABOUT 5 FRONT

2. **No plan**. When a rider has no plan at all, he is simply working from his thoughts and ideas. "Get through Turn 6 faster" **is not a plan, it is merely an idea**. It might be based on the thought that your being passed in that turn, or that you're just not going fast enough. In this case, No

Plan = No Result. You can't know whether your plan worked out if you didn't have a plan to begin with. That's not the real problem with having no plan, though. The real problem is that the rider hasn't decided where his attention will be well-spent, so he spends it on everything and anything that comes up.

With no plan, you sample the motion, but you don't have enough thoughts to judge your progress.

The most classic No-Plan situation is the one that goes: "I'm just going out to ride as hard as I can!" What that means is that the rider is going to go out on the track and find his extremes of corner speed, traction, braking, steering and such: The rider is working with an **idea** but no plan. He's braking into a turn, and all of his attention is on the idea of extreme braking. Then, each in its turn, he shifts over to the ideas of extreme lean angle, extreme corner speed and last, to extreme acceleration off the turn.

There isn't anything particularly wrong with braking as hard as you can, leaning over to the maximum, having the highest corner speed possible and getting a really great drive, providing that's what is needed for any given turn. What's wrong is that no plan exists to put those ideas into place with the smooth transitions to see that they work out.

Most riders never take their thoughts past the idea stage to form a plan.

When you're paid to win you have to hang it out, even in practice.

I try to keep up an idea exchange with my mechanics so I can be open to their input. Maybe the bike can be set up better to handle some problem.

Two plans operating at the same time creates disorder.

3. **Two plans.** Having two or more plans for any one turn or section of track is one of the all-time favorite mistakes. It is also one of the most difficult ways to ride, and definitely creates many more problems than the rider can easily solve while riding. Let's look at how it works.

As illustration, let's say your job was to put stock on the shelves of a small grocery store. Two men own the store; both men can give you instructions, and either can fire you. One of the owners wants you to work very fast, stacking the cans any which way — just get them on the shelves. The other owner likes you to stack the cans in neat patterns that take a lot of time to arrange. They walk by and check your work every 15 minutes, each of them critizing you for doing your work the wrong way. As you react to their two different **plans**, some of the cans will be stacked neatly and some will be in disorder. In the same way, if you are riding with two different plans, your riding will be in disorder too.

Let's take an example closer to the track. You get the **idea** that you're supposed to brake deep into turns. You also get the idea that to be good, you need to be smooth. You go out and practice hard braking until you can lift the rear wheel off the ground going into any turn, the hardest possible braking that can be done on your bike. Every time you do this, you find that at the end of braking, you have so much **attention** on it that you miss your turn-entry point and run wide, or have to make a rough steering change. And when you do this, the bike bobbles under the rough handling and you have to slow down more to get in the turn.

That's No Plan

The first thing, of course, is that "going in deep" and "being smooth" are ideas, not plans. If you have been racing, you can supply yourself with many examples of this kind of situation, I'm sure. The point is that **you have two ideas operating at once, and they fight each other**. And using two plans such as the Drive Plan and the Wide Arc Plan (see Chapter X) at the same time will really get you into trouble, because the two are completely different.

Two Plans Evolve

The way two or more plans usually come about is when a rider finds some dissatisfaction with one, then decides to correct that turn or track section with another. The original plan was never fully abandoned; the rider simply stacks one on top of the first. He is, in effect, taking orders from two bosses, and he can't fully satisfy either of them.

That is not to say that you shouldn't have an **alternate plan** to get around some turn.

The stock boy must learn how to stack cans fast and neatly to keep his job, which requires some skill and patience. You must do the same in riding to avoid the two-plan conflict.

4. **A plan with no action**. This mistake can come in two forms:
   a) You never try the new plan you came up with. You continue the old one with no change.
   b) You never thought out the changes you would have to make in your riding to make the new plan work, so it doesn't. You could say that b) is really the cause of a).

If, for instance, you decided to get a better drive off a turn, and to do it you have to go in deeper before turning, but you don't find another Reference Point on the track to signal you when to turn, you will automatically revert to the old way of doing it. You never get a chance to try the new plan. **The thoughts for the plan were there, but no motion, or changes in motion, were included.**

When a rider changes plans, he has to change the thoughts and ideas that go together to form that plan.

5. **Trimming the Christmas Tree**. One of the first things you are likely to hear when you first come to a track is: "I haven't got my line down in Turn __," or, "I'm trying to find my line in such and such a turn," or

If you have a bad feeling about a turn, go through it slower and try to figure it out.

worse, "What line do you use through Turn __?" All of these statements or questions lead to the idea that getting some line and keeping it is the answer to any problem in any turn. It has become part of the racetrack patter, and it is a trap to some extent, if you continue to think that way.

The trap is finding a line (**plan**) through any section, and then "robotically" repeating it until you become so committed to it that you're unable to change. At that point, your riding feels a little out of control, or as if you were doing something you didn't really want to do.

It's really very simple: if you don't feel that you can change something, you won't.

Now, you are running into one of those things that often plague a rider — wanting to change and not being able to.

If you have bad feelings about a turn or set of turns, don't push it. But you also have to look at it as a challenge, something to overcome.

An overdone plan is a different problem.

Christmas Tree Problem

Here is the problem and how it develops. You find a "line" and become stuck to it. How do you become stuck on a line? You make a great **plan** to get through a turn, and you do it in practice. Everything works great, you are set up right, with good control, and you know where you are and what you want to do. Perfect. Then, like decorating a **Christmas Tree**, you begin to hang ornaments on the plan. Maybe you can push it a little harder at the entrance, lean it just a little more in the middle, begin the drive just a little sooner, brake a little deeper into the steering action, go through one gear higher. The list of "ornaments" is almost endless. And, just like with a Christmas Tree, after all the ornaments have been hung — all the icicles, angel hair, artificial snow, lights, candy canes, greeting cards, tinsel, stars and the rest of it — you can't see the tree anymore.

Dirt track is half the things to think about, two turns, two straights. There aren't too many lines on a dirt track but on a road course, you can go anywhere. Road racing is much more of a science because of that choice.

Precious Plan

Like the Christmas Tree, you become snowed in with all the details of the plan. You get so involved with the details that you stop working with the original, and just concentrate on the parts you can see. The worst of it is that when a rider has so much work in something, he is unlikely to give it up. The Christmas Tree becomes so precious that you are afraid to change anything on it. Do you have a turn you ride like that? Let's see if we can find a way out.

Plan/Turn Checklist

Here is a checklist for you to use on every turn of the track. You should tab this page and use it to go over each turn at some point. Don't ignore using it "after" the race. You don't want to forget everything you learned while racing; it will be handy to remember next time. Do the whole checklist for each turn.

1. Do you have a **plan** for this turn?
   (Yes or No?)
2. What is it?
   (Think it through.)
3. Is that a **plan**, a **thought** or an **idea**?
   (A plan takes the whole turn into consideration.)
   (A thought is something you noticed.)
   (An idea is an incomplete plan; something you think you can or can't do.)
4. If it is a plan, what is the current result?
   (Are you able to ride according to the plan?)
5. Does the plan need refinement or changes to work?
   (Decide whether your plan is complete, and make sure you do not have more than one plan.)
6. If you need corrections in the plan, should you correct the thoughts and ideas, or the motion?
   (Is it what you think or what you do that needs fixing?)
7. What other thoughts and ideas do you have for this turn?
   (What else do you notice while riding it?)
8. What part of the motion-speed, lean angle, traction, rpm, etc. are you spending your **attention** on?
   (What part do you notice?)
9. Do the things you notice in 7 and 8 fit into your plans for the turn?
   (Do they add to or subtract from your plan?)
10. Break the turn down by where you are **sampling** the motion and where you are sampling the **thoughts** connected to your **plan**. (The areas where you are unclear on what is being looked at are the areas or things that are either missing from your plan, part of another plan, or the result of having no plan at all.)
11. Do you have **feelings** about some part of the turn that make it hard to ride?
    (Does something in the turn scare you? Did you ever crash in this

turn? Do you remember a time when someone else crashed here?)
12. What about it is easy and feels good?

   If answering these questions doesn't handle any problems you are
having with this turn or turns, try using the Master Checklist in
Chapter XIII.

CHAPTER IV

Motion

What You Do

The bike has to be set up comfortable for you because every track is different.

Motion is described in Webster's Dictionary as "the act or process of changing position." Motion for a motorcycle rider can be divided into two main areas:

1. **What the rider does to operate the bike**.
   a) Rotate the throttle, on and off.
   b) Push and pull the handlebar for steering.
   c) Pull and release the clutch lever.
   d) Pull and release the brake lever.
   e) Pull up and push down on the gear lever.
   f) Change body position on the bike.
   g) Depress rear brake lever (if rear brake is used).
2. **What the bike does in response to the rider's control**.
   a) Change speed.
   b) Turn.

Strange exercises or just changing speed and direction?

Busy, Busy, Busy

As you can see, the rider is the busy beaver in this activity of riding. You can perform as many as **seven actions** on a motorcycle, and you can even do them all at the same time in some cases. But even if you do all seven at once, you can only produce two effects: **Turn** or **change speed**. Everything a rider does on a bike is broken down to these two things. And except for the straightaways, you are always doing both of them.

I have to admit, as you probably will, that most often riding seems much more complicated than that. Now, imagine that you could hook up the controls directly to your thoughts. It would eliminate six of the things you do on a bike. Your only concern would be changing your body position on the seat, and holding onto the bike!

When you change your plan, you either change speed, steering, or both.

Example: You've just come back into the pits after a five-lap practice. In thinking over your riding, you are dissatisfied with what was happening in "Turn 9." What was wrong?

1. Your speed through the turn?

2. Where the bike was on the track (the result of where you turned it)?

3. A combination of speed and steering?

Don't bother to look anywhere else; those are your only choices.

There is nothing else you can change.

Note: We are assuming that the bike is not giving you any problems; it is working well.

Plans To Change

All right, you think it over and you decide that because there was still some track available on the turn's exit (the result of your **steering**), you should be able to go add **speed** toward the exit of Turn 9. From your original **plan**; only one thing has changed. Where you positioned the bike on the track was OK, so you don't change that. You only have to change the speed. The obvious limitations you must deal with, of course, don't change. The bike's Lean Angle Ground Clearance to max and the Tire Traction are your two limiting factors. Now you work out your plan to determine how to make the speed change.

1. Where will you begin to increase speed?
2. How much will you increase it?
3. What will this speed change look like, and how will it feel?

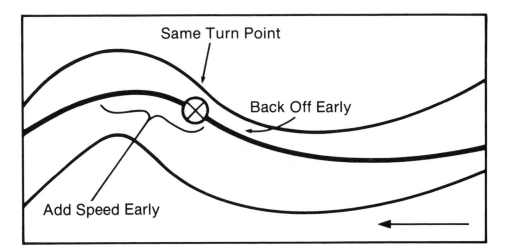

A basic plan includes speed and direction changes.

Too Many Changes

Work on the things you're scared about, blind about or don't know. Don't try and change 5 things in one practice it's too many.

When you make a change in your plan, never change more than one thing at a time.

Riders almost always try to change too many things at once. Think over your own riding to see if you don't usually decide to change your speed along with your line. Now, look at the situation from a more scientific point of view. If you change both speed and steering (line), you won't know which one — or if both — produced the result you get, good or bad.

Be Nice To The Rider

Riding already seems complicated enough; don't make it any harder than it has to be. In our Turn 9 example, you go out in the next practice and make that one "minor" adjustment to your **plan**. You have kept the task simple by doing everything the same except for working out the throttle changes to increase the speed. Changing just that one thing will leave you enough **attention** to work this new **idea** into your already established **plan**. You'll spend a lot of attention on **sampling** speed, because that's what you're changing. Obviously, you still need to pay attention to where you're going (steering), but you should choose to spend more on the speed change, for now, to see how it works out.

Whatever you change will always demand more of your attention.

If you change something because you make a mistake, the same holds true. You pay a lot of attention to it, because it wasn't planned for.

All The Changes

All the changes you can make are speed and steering changes. Your choice of how to adjust them are limited to these:

1. **Speed** (How much you do of each of the following):
   a.) Accelerate
   b.) Decelerate
   c.) Hold a constant speed

Note: To hold a constant speed in a turn, it's necessary to make throttle changes because the turn itself slows the bike. In an uphill turn, even more throttle has to be used. It would be possible to hold a constant speed in a long sweeper, but you usually accelerate through those, anyway.

2. **Steering**
   a) Where you steer (where you turn the bike)
   b) How much you steer (how tight you make a turn)

So, breaking this process down one step further, you have exact changes you can make on the bike in order to work out your **plan**. From another viewpoint, **speed and steering are the things you plan for**.

The Limit

The things that are complicated about riding are things that limit the two factors of motion.

Speed is limited on both ends of the scale — how fast you can accelerate and how fast you can slow down. Too much acceleration and you can spin the wheel. Too much brake and you lock it up.

Steering is limited by how far you can lean the bike over, and by how fast you can achieve the desired lean angle. If you lean it over too far, you run off the tires or drag the bike's undercarriage. If you steer it too quickly, the bike can slide. Both Steering and Speed are limited by Traction (see Chapter VII).

Plans And Motion

While working on your riding, you must only consider speed and steering.

Both factors are limited by **traction**. Deciding to change your speed at some point will affect your steering, and changing your steering will affect how much speed you can use. The important thing to remember is to keep speed and steering as isolated from each other as possible. Take our Turn 9 example again. You came out of the turn and found you still had track space you could use. An **idea** occurred to you: "I can exit this turn faster; there is still room." You set up a **plan** to add speed coming out of the turn. Your plan changes only the speed, not the place where you steer the machine or the amount you turn it.

A plan to change speed. Good. Don't change the steering yet.

Try The Plan

The next step is to try the **plan**. By isolating one factor, **speed**, you make as few changes as possible. You put as much of your **attention** on the speed change as you can, then find out what happens. If all goes well, you come out of the turn faster, and use up all of the track space you had left over when you exited at a lower speed. That unused track space is the limiting factor to how fast you could come off that turn using the speeds and steering factors of your plan. Now you've got something that works, and you should practice it until sticking to the plan is easy. **Maybe it only takes you two laps to fit everything together; maybe it takes 10.**

Push The Limit

It's hard trying to find the max lean angle. There's a lot more important than seeing how far you can lean it. If you lean it over more you usually skid both ends. You only lean it over all the way if you're going to run it off the track.

Now you're in a position to work on the last factor, **traction**. You've got a **plan**, and now it's time to check out your plan's limits. Once again, you carefully begin adding some speed to each part of the turn until you find the traction limits of your plan. A word of caution: Find the limits at a rate that's comfortable for you. **Plan where you will go faster.** Don't fall into the old trap of just gassing it up; add speed a little bit at a time, and at the places where you choose.

Remember: A turn can always be broken into at least three parts: Entry, Middle and Exit. If increased speed is the idea, decide which part you want to work on. Attack all three at once, and it may be more than you can do easily.

More Plans To Change

Steering changes are more difficult than speed changes.

The reason I've left **steering** until last is that steering changes will require major revisions in your **plan** because they take more time and more track to put into effect. A speed change can be done with a simple wrist motion; a steering change takes longer, and must be planned for well in advance.

Basically Steering

Where you turn starts the whole thing off.

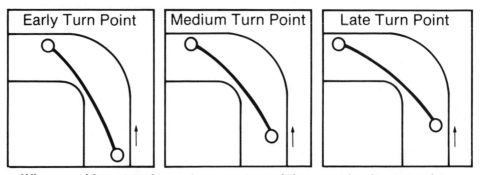

| Early Turn Point | Medium Turn Point | Late Turn Point |

Where and how much you turn are two of the most basic parts of your plan.

Once you have the overall plan for a turn, the very first thing you have to do is find the places on the track to steer the bike in order to make the plan work.

Where you steer the bike is like the frame of the machine. The engineer has an overall plan to make the motorcycle. He wants it to do certain things and he wants it to look a certain way. The first thing he designs is the frame. The frame will carry all of his **ideas**, and is the backbone of the overall plan. The frame design will determine how much power the engine can have, how wide the wheels will be, how sticky a tire can be used and much more.

Where you will steer is the frame for your plan.

Where you steer determines:
1. How much speed can be used.
2. Where you must be on the track (before making a turn).

3. Your track position (after you initiate a turn).
4. How much braking you can do.
5. Where your braking will end.
6. Where you can change gears.
7. What your body position on the bike should be.
8. How far you lean the bike.

   You don't have to stretch your imagination very far to see that this is an extremely critical part of your **plan**. Where you steer affects everything else you do in the turn to a large degree.

   Look back over your own riding. Just how accurate have you been with this important step?

All Of The Senses

   Take an even closer look at where you steer and you will see that all the 5 senses of riding come into play.
   1. Speed. Your turn entry-speed and turn speed itself will be affected by where you steer it into the turn.
   2. Traction. How quickly you turn will have a direct result in how much traction your tires will have. Turning in gradually will give you more traction possibilities than turning in quickly.
   3. Timing. The exact point where you do the steering is the subject we are discussing.
   4. Lean Angle Ground Clearance. Your LAGC will be determined by where you turn the bike. For instance, you will have to lean it more to begin with if you go in deeper before turning than you would if you started turning sooner.
   5. Location. Your line and direction through the turn will be affected by where you turn. Turning sooner will generally make the bike run wider at the exit. Turning later generally gives you a tighter exit.

Argument

   You can look at this in many ways and perhaps have already figured out that any of the 5 senses could be the basis for all of the rest.
   You can argue that your idea of speed and how fast you wanted to enter or go through the turn would determine where you would start it. That is true.
   You can also argue that where and how fast you turn would have to be set by how well your tires worked, your sense of traction and ability to use what you have. That is true as well.
   It can be argued that the limitations of your machine in terms of LAGC would also be the determining factor in steering. True as well.
   Lastly, you could say that your line or location would really be the major factor in turning point for any turn. That is also very true. To get a certain line through a turn you would have to pay attention to the turn point.
   So what is the answer to this riddle? If everything determines everything, how do you figure it out?

The Turning Solution

The answer is truly simple. To improve, you must start from somewhere and your Turning Point is a definite and exact thing you can do on the track. You can know, by direct observation, whether or not you turned at the "second crack in the pavement."

You can see with your own eyes how it affects your progress through the turn: Your line.

You can decide, with a high degree of accuracy, if you need to lean it over more or not, come in with more speed or less, or make suspension adjustments for more traction or stability.

In short, you set up a framework for devising a **plan**. A framework that can be easily observed to work or not, **with an exact beginning**.

Help

Here is one of the few ways you can actually let someone help you with your riding besides having them take accurate lap times.

It is simple and may help. Just have your friend go out and see if you are turning at the same point each time you come up to some particular turn. Get an outside observer's point of view on it.

What does that do? It just drills you to become accurate and you will find that after a while it doesn't take much of your **attention** to hit that turning point and you will have some **attention** left over to ride!

Note: Knowing where you are so that you can set up this framework is the only piece of information you will need and that is the subject of the next chapter.

Chapter Recap

1. While the rider may be involved in up to seven different control actions, the only two effects he can create on a motorcycle are to change its **speed** or **direction**.
2. From the point of view of improvement, you only have to look at those two factors to see what you need to change to make any turn better for you.
3. When making a speed change you should first think out the three factors that will make it work or not:
   a. Where you will begin to make the change.
   b. How much you will change it.
   c. What the end result will look like or feel like to you.
4. When making a change on the track, in steering or in speed, you should plan to spend more of your attention on it because it will take more to get it right.
5. Your **plan** is composed of speed and steering changes.
6. The major limiting factor in speed and steering changes is Traction.
7. Making one change, either in speed or in steering, at a time will help you narrow down the changes that work out. Changing both at once can become complicated and you probably won't learn as much.

8. Throttle changes are easier to make than steering changes but you should not fall into the trap of just gassing it up as hard as you can. Bring the speed up a little at a time. Use the throttle as a fine tuning device rather than an axe.

9. Where you steer or begin the turn is the framework of your **plan** and has a huge effect on everything that happens after that in the turn.

10. Your Turning Point involves all of the 5 senses of riding and can determine how much you use each of them.

11. It can easily be argued that any of the 5 senses can be the keystone to your riding in a turn. Each of them could be thought to be the major factor of any **plan**.

12. The reason for using your Turning Point as the key factor in a turn is that you can directly observe the results of your efforts. You can even have someone else watch you in a turn and decide whether you were being accurate or not.

13. The purpose of becoming accurate on a race track is simply to free up your **attention** so you can do more things easier.

Questions and Drills

1. What turn do you have the most trouble with on this track? (On some other track?)
   a) Do you have an accurate turning-in point for it? (On some other track?)
   b) Could a more precise Turn Point help?
   c) Is it some other problem with this turn?

2. What turn do you do the best or like the best?
   a) Do you have a good Turn Point?
   b) Did you get so accurate with this turn that you can turn almost anywhere you want and still have it work out?
   c) Could a more accurate Turn Point help even more?

3. Do Speed changes take up a lot of your **attention**?
   a) Do you find yourself making a lot of throttle changes in some turn or another?
   b) Is there really a good reason for those changes?
   c) Is it something you feel forced to do?
   d) Did you ever try leaving the throttle alone?

4. In the past, have you noticed yourself making both Speed and Steering changes in turns you were working out?
   a) Did you ever try to change only one of those at a time?
   b) Can you see that it is more complicated to change both at the same time?
   c) Do you think you can change both anyhow?

5. In the turn you have the most trouble with, is the trouble:
   a) The speed you are going (too slow or too fast)?
   b) Where you are on the track (too wide, too tight or lost)?

6. When you make a steering or speed change, do you:
   a) Decide how you will start it?
      (Do you find a reference point on the track to make this

change?) (Do you think out how you will actually turn the throttle or move the bars to make it work?)

b) Figure out what it will change from how you were doing it before. (Will you need to lean it over more?) (Is the speed going to be greater so that you will actually need more traction and not lean it over as much?) Will a sharper steering change make traction a problem?) Etc., etc.

c) Try and get a feeling of how the whole turn will go from the changes you will make? (Will going faster change the exit too much?) (Is the middle of the turn going to require any big changes in steering or speed?) (Will your drive suffer because you are too wide or have it leaned over too far?) Etc., etc.

7. Have you spent any time thinking about speed and steering changes or are you just reading through this material to find the tricks?

NOTES

CHAPTER V

Location

My Current Address Is:
The Corkscrew, Laguna Seca, Planet Earth!

This one is the plan! If you don't know where you want to be at the exit when you are actually riding, with everything speeded up, you won't get it.

Your most basic **concern** while riding is **location** — where you are on the track. The use of **reference points** (RPs) is pretty well covered in "A Twist of the Wrist," and it's unnecessary to cover the whole subject again here. There are, however, some small twists to that subject which have come up over the years since that book was written which might be of help to you.

Location Limits

Before you go about adding any frills to your riding, such as traction limits, speed limits, precision timing or exploring the lean angle limits, the thing that is likely to concern you most is **location**.

"I'm just going out to find where the track goes," is one of the first things you're likely to hear from a rider at a new track. That's because the rest of the **5 senses** of riding are usually sidelined until you feel comfortable with the turns.

Even though **traction** is the major limiting factor in speed and steering changes, your own Location on the track comes first. **Speed, lean angle, timing and traction can only be explored after you know where you are**.

What Now?

To apply the **idea of location** to learning a track, you can divide the problem into two main areas:
1. Turn layout (how the turn is constructed).
2. Rider's location, and the direction or line to best handle the track situation for his style of riding.

With all of the fat trimmed off, the great majority of riding can be expressed in two questions: "Where am I on the track?" and "What does my **location** mean I should do?" All of the actions of riding are based on the second question, which is, in turn, based on the first.

How Much And When?

Serious riding begins when you address two more questions: "How much?" and "When?"

How much traction, how much speed, how much steering or lean angle you should use — and when you will do it — all depend on location.

Sharpshooter

You've got to know where the target is before you can pull the trigger and hit the bull's-eye. As a result, one of the first things you learn in shooting is to keep your eyes on the target. Once you have the feel of the gun in your hands, you can begin to make adjustments in how you hold it, how you squeeze the trigger and so on. As you become more experienced, you can change how you hold and adjust the gun, but you never change one basic part: Keep your eyes on the target. For a shooter, that's the basic drill to handle **location**.

Racing, with its added dimension of **motion**, is more like shooting clay pigeons than paper targets. You watch the moving target, sure, but you place your shots a little ahead of it. You "lead" the target while it is in flight. By doing that, you take several things into consideration:

1. Where the target is now.
2. What direction it's going.
3. Where it will be in the near future (the next ½ second or so).

Pulling the trigger at the right time — and consequently hitting the moving target — depend on getting those factors of **location** correct. When you're riding, you are providing the motion, but the same three considerations still apply:

1. Where am I now?
2. What direction am I going?
3. Where will I be next?

You "lead" the bike around the track based on what you see in front of you and what you do with the controls to handle that situation. Those three factors of **location** are the basis for all your decisions about riding.

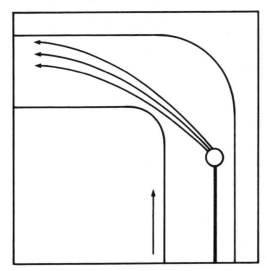

"What direction is it going, exactly?"

Attention To Location

"Too much attention on current location and you lose track of direction and future location."

All three of the above are important to you while riding, but having your **attention** stuck on any one of them for very long will get you in as much trouble as you think it will get you out of. Here is what can happen:

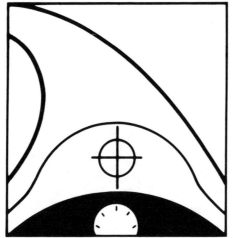

1. Spending all of your **attention** on where you are at any given moment can make you lose track of your **direction** and **future location**.

Example: You have a good **reference point** that's easy to see, right at the apex of a turn. As you approach it, your attention is on it. You forget to look further ahead in the turn until you reach your RP. You are travelling at race speed, which means the track is going by at perhaps more than 100 feet per second. You roll the gas off because you haven't prepared for the next section of the turn, you're "lost."

On the other hand, forgetting to keep track of where you are "now" will make you lose track of what you should be doing with the controls. You can easily lose your **sense of timing** by getting ahead of yourself.

"Too much attention on direction but no exact future location is not precise enough."

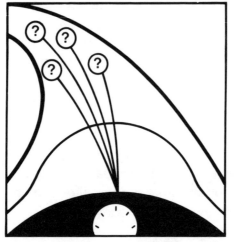

2. Spending all of your **attention** on your **direction**, without having a particular destination in mind — a **future location** — will get you "somewhere over there." Not very accurate or confidence inspiring.

Example: You've just entered a well-banked turn at say 75 mph. You can't really see the edge of the track at the end of the turn. You sort of "point" the bike in that direction. You don't have an accurate place to aim for, which gives you the uncertain feeling that the line you're on could be easily 2-3 feet off, maybe all the way off the course. You hesitate with your drive until you can see where you're going to wind up. You don't have control of the situation; you're just waiting to see what's going to happen. Does this seem familiar?

This situation has an opposite side to it, too. If you don't spend some **attention** on your direction of travel, you can have an accurate exit point in mind for a turn, but you won't be able to reach it because you simply weren't paying enough attention to your progress through the turn. You see that exit point or mid-turn reference point, but as you approach it you find yourself on the wrong part of the track, usually too wide. It happens to riders all the time. Has it ever happened to you?

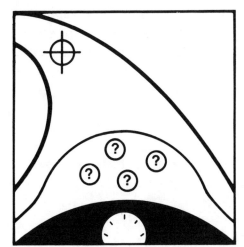

3. Spending all of your **attention** on **future location** can make you lose both your **timing points** and the exact **direction** you're going.

Example: You approach a turn going a bit faster than you've ridden it before. Your ability to predict what is going to happen when you arrive in the turn is poor because you have no experience with it at this speed. You become a little anxious about that and focus all of your **attention** up ahead in the turn. As a result, you miss your turning point. You didn't pay enough attention to it, you were spending it elsewhere.

"Too much attention on future location will lose your timing points and direction."

Some things, like the drive, are really important. You start spending on them before you get there.

Speed Experiments

The most common error in racing is to turn in too soon when you're experimenting with speed.

End-of-braking markers, turning points and throttle control can all go up in smoke on the entry to a turn if you begin to "look into" the turn too soon, and it's almost always the result of trying to use more speed going in. The extra speed puts your **attention** on **future location**.

The flip side of this condition is fairly obvious. If you don't have some attention on **future location**, you won't know whether your **current direction** is getting you where you want to go, or whether your control actions are going to work out or how.

That, of course, is **timing**, and part of timing is seeing ahead to judge where your present actions will put you on the track. You know how this works: You turn the throttle on a bit more than last lap, and then desperately look ahead to see if you have enough track available to use that extra speed. Right?

Past Location

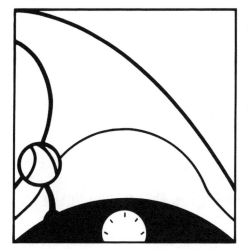

Actually, there is a fourth problem, too. Some riders can't help reviewing the turn they just went through which is a **past location**. In an attempt to work out what was good or bad about the turn they just completed, their **attention** becomes stuck there.

"After" you've completed a turn, if you have a straigthaway where you can spend some time to reflect on the last turn, doing so is OK. In fact, reviewing the turn you just completed while it's still fresh in your mind is

"Your attention can become stuck on past location."

probably the best time to do it. If you had to spend all of your attention on just riding that turn, right afterward would be the best time to review it. It can, obviously, become a problem if you're still contemplating that turn when you need to be doing something else — like setting up for the next one.

Ideal Location

The perfect situation for a rider would be to keep all three factors of **location** under control.
1. Where am I now?
2. What direction am I going?
3. Where will I be next?

Control over location equals knowing where you are, what direction you're moving in and where you will be.

Locations Arguments

I've had some trouble breaking down **location**, because in some turns it seems easy to see where you're going but hard to get there. It seemed like having some **reference point** or spot to shoot for on the track would be all that was needed. Riders would have a spot picked out on the exit of some turn, then find that as they drew nearer to it (especially in fast turns where you can't make much of a steering change), they weren't going to hit the spot. It creates some considerable confusion for the rider. I've done some experimenting, and came up with an analysis: **Riders having problems attaining a consistent line in turns make their steering change, then forget about direction.**

Don't get me wrong; ideally, that would be just the way to do it. You'd approach the turn, lean the bike in at just the right place and get exactly the line you wanted. You'd be sure it was perfect from the beginning. Then, you'd have all your **attention** free to **sample traction, speed** and your **control timing**. In fact, the best riders ride just this way, especially in fast turns. The ability to get the direction of the bike set right and quickly from the beginning makes a huge difference in how the turn works out. It's one of the things that separates the good riders from the mediocre. If you can do this and still go fast, you are well on your way to becoming a good rider. Can you?

Locate The Parts

Turns don't come ready-made with established **entrances, middles** and **exits. Where you make the control actions marks those places for you**.

Generally, the **entrance** is that part of the turn where braking is completed and turning is initiated. The **middle** is the part of the turn that begins when the throttle is turned on again. The middle ends and the **exit** begins where the drive starts.

In some turns you can dispense with the middle and go right to the

Riding a 500 really makes a superbike or a 250 easier because you have to be more precise with the 500's.

"Where is the entrance of this turn for you?" All of them can work.

exit depending on how you handle the turn. You eliminate the section of the turn with few or no speed adjustments in it. That's OK, because it really makes the turn much simpler. Then, the turn is just entrance and exit. Unfortunately, you can't reduce all turns to the two-step type — certainly not the long ones.

Of course, we've returned to the fact that each rider sees the track from his own **ideas** on how it should be ridden, what he should be doing and what will work in a particular type of turn.

If someone says, "I go deep into the entrance of Turn 6, and lean over to the pegs," you are still faced with your own mental picture of just what "deep into Turn 6" is. On the other hand, if someone says, "Run it into the pavement patch about 2 feet from the edge of the track," you know what he means by "going deep."

From a theoretical point of view, having the entrance and the middle be as short as possible — and the exit as long as possible — is the fastest way around any turn.

Don't spend alot of time in the middle, get in and get out. It doesn't work everywhere but it's basically the right idea for most turns except big sweepers.

"Having the entry and middle be as short as possible is an idea. Can it be done in every turn?"

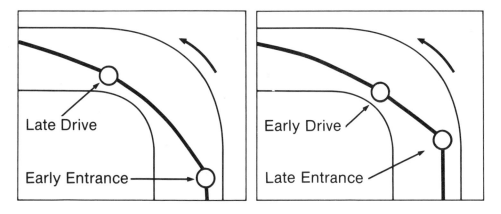

Late Drive

Early Entrance

Early Drive

Late Entrance

51

You'd spend as little time as you could on the steering and the part where you hold a constant speed or make small speed adjustments, and the most time and space on the drive out of the turn, where you're rolling on the throttle.

Watch how quickly the steering changes are made by the world's best riders. You'll rarely see them slowly "bending" the bike into the turns. They reach the point where they want to start turning and it's done. When you work up to making steering changes that fast, you need to make them at the right point on the track. The entrance of a turn for a Freddie or an Eddie or a Kenny is a very short experience in terms of steering. How often do you practice quick and accurate steering? If you don't do it enough, you might find that your steering point isn't accurate. Attaining accuracy in your steering point is the first step in trying quick steering changes.

"Your own idea of how it should be is the SAMPLING procedure."

Too Late

Perfect

Too Early

Free Sample

Location is a thought process. Where you are in a turn means something to you. How you achieve your **location** is based on **ideas** you have about where you should be and what you should be doing.

You keep track of your location in a turn by sampling.

You spot some familiar turn or pavement, then match that with your **idea** of where you believe you should be. Either you're sure of where you are or you aren't. You either have a good **idea** of what you should be doing there or you don't. If you find yourself waiting for something to happen, it won't.

Note: This doesn't mean you can't relax on a bike. But being relaxed is the result of knowing what you should be doing and where you are. When you are relaxed in a turn at race speed, you are **sampling** the results of what you did, and you're working out what will happen. That extreme concentration on sampling is the hard part of racing. It is also the fun part. There is no free sample; it all costs.

The whole point in getting your **location** straight to begin with is so you can free up your **attention** for other important parts of riding: Speed, traction, lean angle and timing.

The goal in figuring out your location is to spend the least amount of attention possible on where you are, not the most.

Working It Out

While you're working on a turn, developing your **plan** on how to do it, all three of the **location factors** must be taken into account.

1. **Current location** — where you are at any given time.
2. **Direction of travel** — the angle your line is cutting through the turn.
3. **Future location** — your ability to judge where you will be at the next instant, or when you'll be at some other part of the turn.

Usually, when riders talk about location, they only address direction.
They discuss their line through a turn which describes what direction they travelled through that turn. That's fine. The overall attempt is to find some consistent way to handle the turn. Watching the best riders go through a turn within a few inches of the same point each time should give you the idea that consistency is a big part of riding.

The use of **reference points**, or having a really good overall picture of a turn, is a key factor in keeping track of the above points. This ability to keep track of your location puts you in control of it.

As you ride a turn and become familiar with it, you name its parts (entrance, middle and exit), so you can judge the three factors of - **location**. You **sample** your location to make certain of where you are going and what you should be doing. If you're having trouble working out a turn, go back to the basic building block — **location** — to make sure you have all three factors straight.

The Line Machine

A training device that marked the pavement each time a rider went through a turn would be a tremendous help. As you approached a section, you'd be able to see exactly where you were on the previous lap. It would help you to remember how the turn worked out, and you could easily make any changes in your methods to help you get through the turn faster.

It seems like you wind up spending the same amount on everything once you get a turn sorted out. Some things take the same amount of attention but you spend more time on them.

How precise do you really have to be?

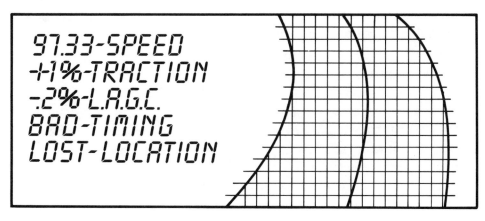

97.33-SPEED
+1%-TRACTION
-.2%-L.A.G.C.
BAD-TIMING
LOST-LOCATION

Taking this thought one step further, the perfect training device would put down a line that would change color with different throttle settings, so you could see the **control timing** you used. To top it off, you could have the line machine show you where the bike lost traction on any given lap. To make such a device perfect, it would be hooked up to a computer that would time each lap, and display the fastest line. The device would also indicate how much faster or slower you were travelling at each part of the track, so you should be able to compare one lap to another. And to make the trainer complete, it would include a helmet-mounted, variable-tone beeper that would track your lean angle. Perhaps a pleasant hum would start when you were within one degree or so of what you did last time.

Such a device would keep track of your **location, timing, traction, speed** and **lean angle**. It would show you the best pass you made on any turn, and it would show you exactly how you did it. Using such a device would probably make you the most consistent rider in the world in a very short time. Too bad it doesn't exist — or does it?

You Are The Machine

Of course, you keep track of all those factors yourself. You make all of those decisions about **thought** and **motion** all the time as you ride. You **sample** each of those factors and make judgments on them as you ride. On top of all that, you record it all for future reference. You already have all of the equipment necessary to make this happen; you only have to sharpen it up. **The fuel you use to drive this machine is your attention.**

Location Again

If you strip away most of the functions of the Line Machine and only had it show you your line from the last lap, it would be simple for you to add most of the other components to that turn. You would be able to spend a lot of **attention** on all of them: Speed, traction, lean angle and timing. If you know exactly what your **location** should be, any turn would be much easier to ride.

The same doesn't hold true for the other 4 **riding senses**. Look at it; you could have indications for speed or traction or timing or lean angle on the track, and you could still be lost in one way or another.

Knowing where you are and where you are going is the cornerstone for building a consistent plan for any turn.

Another Line

There's another way of considering a line: It's the result of what you did to control the bike. Where you turned, how much speed you had or how hard you were accelerating, the result of a slide, and your lean angle, all determine your **line**.

If you take your present location and the next place you'll be, then connect them, you will have the line. On a roadrace track, you always

It's better to be going slow and know where you are than fast and not know.

have those two things to consider, current position and your intended position farther along. Without both of those parts, you don't have a line.

How you got to the place you wind up at will be determined by how much you change your **speed** and **direction**. Adding too much speed will certainly change your final position on the track. Not enough steering at the beginning of a turn and you'll run a different line than before. Do you wind up where you want to be? Do you frequently find yourself in different spots in the same turns on different laps?

When your idea of where you want to be determines what you do with the controls, you have a line. When what you do with the controls determines where you are, the line has you.

Line Adjustments

Current location tells you what you should be doing to get your future location. While you're in a turn, one of the big reasons you don't just roll on the gas more and more is that you don't want to run out of track at the exit. In a series of turns or **esses**, you'll need to set up for the next turn; you have another destination or location to get to before you reach your final place in that set of turns. You have your **idea** of your final destination, and you want it to be part of the track that has asphalt on it, not dirt.

Having that final point in mind will tell you everything you need to know about adjusting your speed and steering. If you know where you are and where you want to be, you can make decisions that will get you to the right point. **If you don't have your location dialed in, you can't make those decisions and changes accurately.**

Fast bike riders have to have it pointed before they get in. With a 250 you have more choices, mostly because of the power. The 250's don't slide as easy.

Backing it off makes it turn easier by weighting the front.

"Current location should always be an indicator for a future location."

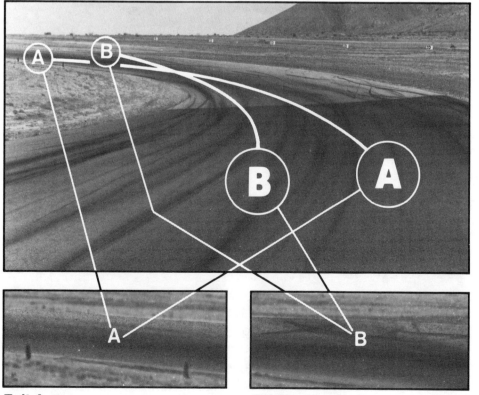

Exit Area   **Off The Track**

Slide Line

These days, everyone is fascinated with sliding roadrace bikes; the controlled slide has become the technique used by the world's best. Most riders are lazy. They just want to charge into turns and have a great line work out from that point on with no big changes. There's nothing really wrong with that technique, since consistency is, after all, part of the goal. But consider what you'd have to do to fit **sliding** into your **location control** (line) while in a turn.

Note: We're talking about "rear" wheel slides in which the back of the bike loses traction somewhat and moves to the outside of a turn.

Each time the bike slides, you've changed direction to some degree. The best slides, obviously, are controllable; they happen when you want them to and to the exact degree you want. If you were using the Line Machine described earlier to record a **slide line**, your **future location** on the track would be indicated by a line with interesting little kinks everywhere you slid the last time through that corner. To reach that future location, you'd "have to" slide the bike.

Example: If you have the bike leaned over all the way, and you have a line set up that uses the entire track along with maximum speed and a **steering slide** built into it, you either slide the bike, slow down, or go off the track.

Slides alter the direction you are going and the line you will run.

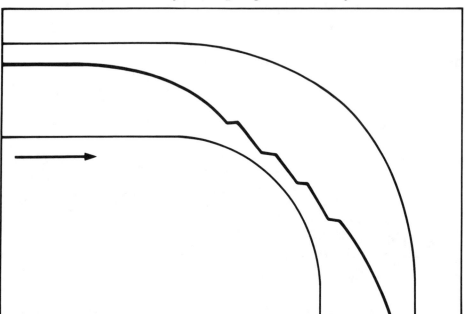

A lot of things come with sliding, if you aren't comfortable with it.

"A series of small slides might look something like this. The resulting line could look very smooth. How 'smooth' would it feel?"

Slide Reactions

If your only reaction to a slide is to roll off the gas or leave the gas on, you're not seeing the whole situation. If you have an unexpected slide in mid-turn, you've just made the exit of that turn more suitable for a better drive out. The bike is turned more toward the inside of the turn which gives you more room on the exit. More room can produce a better drive by effectively making the track wider.

The rider who understands the actual result of a slide can usually make more time at the exit than the amount he lost in the middle because of the slide.

Sliding brings up some important points about the rest of the turn, and most of them can be used to your advantage. **Speed** can be increased as a result of controlled sliding. So can **traction** because you'll be able to pick the bike up a little more, allowing more tire contact on the road and a decreased lean angle. A controlled slide affects **timing**, as well, because you're in the position to start your drive a little sooner. Each of these factors is affected by a slide-induced change in direction.

There's 'no traction' at max lean angle.

Drive Changes

Consider the best riders on high-horsepower bikes: They spin the bike's rear wheel coming off some turns. Two things are happening when they do:

1. The wheel spin seems to propel them out of the turn faster than a perfectly "hooked up" tire would.

2. The back end "comes around" enough to allow them to use the extra drive they get from the spinning wheel.

The sliding wheel isn't always a benefit, though. The big exception is a **front-wheel slide**. You lose track space from a front-wheel slide because the front of the bike points towards the outside of a turn, just the opposite of a rear-wheel slide. Believe me, no one is very enthusiastic about sliding the front end! Also, if you get really sideways on the exit of a turn while you're in the hard part of your drive out, you can't make up the time you lost.

Esses that have slow entrance and fast exits are important. Like the chicane at Daytona. You've got to be spinning it a little to get it turned but you can't spin it too much or you'll high side it.

Accuracy Drill: Connect-A-Dot

Let's go back to our sharpshooter for a moment. He knows how things are going by watching for holes in his target. That's the **line** for target practice. The shooter shoots, producing a hole — the result of how he handled his gun. The hole either is close to the bull's-eye or it isn't. In much the same way, you ride and come up with a line and a procedure for using your controls on that line. You get a good result — lower lap times, or a bad result — higher times. Motorcycles don't leave holes in the pavement usually, so we have to take this lesson and apply it by using the track surface as a guide.

Once you've decided on how to ride a turn, you find marks on the pavement or some other method of signaling yourself that it is time to make control actions to make your **plan** work. The shooter looks at the holes he just made and decides how to adjust his gun to make the next hole closer to the bull's-eye. The holes are his **reference points**; they tell him what he should do next. Your reference points tell you what to do, too. If, for example, you set up a turning point at the entrance to a turn, you should be able to turn at that point. Not 3 feet before it or 3 feet after it, but right at that point.

Most tracks or turns are similar to some turn at another track.

Fast Points

Look at it this way: The faster you ride, the more accurate your timing must be. If you are riding a turn at maximum speed and lean angles, using up the entire track on the exit, how much difference will it make in your speed through that turn if you miss your turning point by 3 feet? If missing your turning point by that much caused you to go 1 mph slower to compensate, and you missed it on every turn by that much, the cumulative effect would be enormous. On a 10-turn track, you could be as much as 1 second slower than you would have been by making you turn accurately. You might not push everything to its limit right now, but that's no reason you shouldn't be prepared to do it when the time comes.

The more accurate you are with your location on the track, the more confidence you have.

Practice Points

"Finding exact locations on the track to make your changes sets up a real procedure. You will need it when you go faster."

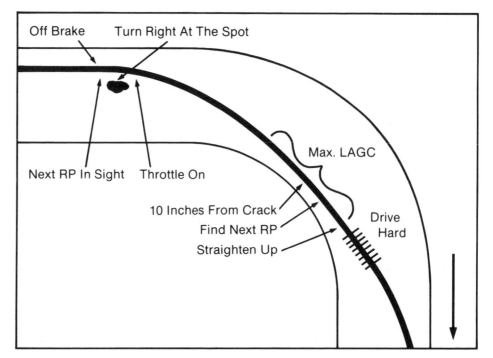

Let's stop fooling around with **accuracy**. Go out and find several points in each turn, like a turning-in point or an end-of-braking marker or the exact place you want to hit the apex and the exit of a turn. Now, hit those spots. Hit them exactly and make the appropriate control action right at that point. If you need some room for error, you've got 2 inches, no more!

If you agree that accuracy is important, you should know that if you can't hit those points at practice speeds, you won't even be close at race speed. Go as slowly as you need to to get them right; whatever speed you can hit them at is the right one for this drill.

Just as the sharpshooter adjusts his sights from a firm rest "before" he needs to make a critical shot, you need to adjust your reference points before the race to make your riding as accurate as it can be.

Changing Points

You can come back with a lot of "what ifs" on this one. What if you're passing, what if your line changes, what if someone drops some oil, what if the shocks fade, what if your tires get greasy, what if your face-shield fogs up, what if you slide unexpectedly, what if you miss a gear, what if . . . ? That list has no end. What if all these things happen at once, what is going to happen to your accuracy? Nothing.

You've got your **reference points**, and you know what you can do if you hit them. **If you don't hit them, you still know where you are.** They give you a very good idea of what you will have to change in order to make the best of things no matter what happens. Being accurate with your location makes your riding tight and forceful. You can be aggressive toward the track and make it work. If you're not accurate on the track, you can still be aggressive, but the result will be sloppy riding that is "soft" and inconsistent.

You can find something out by riding around a track in a car.

Critical Review

While we're on the subject of practice, you can add one more dimension to what you are doing as you set up each turn. You might have heard of riders who practice one turn at a time, and only in qualifying or the race itself do they put everything together. The practice times they get aren't very good. The race times can be very good.

By using the idea of **past location**, and by knowing the places on the track where there's enough time to look over a turn that's just been ridden, you can "set" what was just done in your mind. If you have trouble remembering what you do or where you were in a turn, you will get a lot of benefit from riding your practice sessions like this. The drill is simple.

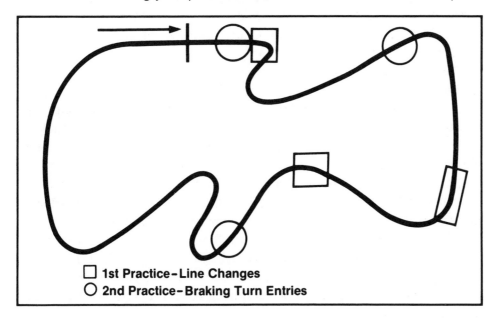

□ 1st Practice – Line Changes
○ 2nd Practice – Braking Turn Entries

Picking particular areas to improve during your practice sessions can add up to better race times."

1. Pick the places on the track where you think there's time to look over a turn just after you ride it. A good example is a turn followed by a straightaway.

2. Without spending **attention** on anything but riding the turn, go out in practice and ride it as hard as you can.

3. Use the time just after you ride that turn to quickly review what you did and where you were as you went through it. If there are two turns in quick succession, or some other situation that won't allow you to spend time reviewing that turn, slow down and make the time. Even if there's a straightaway and you've got the time, slow down so you don't have to pay **attention** to hard acceleration. Just motor along while you're thinking things through.

4. Make a good **mental recording** of what you did and where you were in that turn.

5. Go on to the next turn that you can practice. If you have to miss practicing one or more of the turns because you slowed up and used that time to think things over, pick that one to practice in the next session.

Chapter Recap

1. Knowing where you are in a turn creates the framework for determining your speed, timing points, lean angles and traction — the other 4 senses of riding.

2. An individual's riding style or his plan to handle a turn are based on his knowledge of **location** in the turn.

3. There are basically four questions to location:
a) **Where** am I?
b) **What** should I be doing here?
c) **How much** of it should I be doing?
d) Exactly **when** should it happen?

4. Riding has a lot of similarities to shooting a gun, especially shooting at moving targets. The shooter has to "lead" his target, and the rider has to "lead" his bike. It breaks down into three factors:
a) **Current Location**
b) **The Direction of Travel**
c) **Future Location**

5. The three factors of **location** are each important to you while riding. However, problems can and do occur if your **attention** becomes stuck on any one of them. Ignoring one or more of them can give you the feeling of being "lost."

6. While experimenting with speed, it's important to keep careful track of your **location**. While adding **speed** to some part of a turn, your **attention** can be diverted from location; poor **timing** is often the result.

7. Having your attention on where you have just been — **past location** — can be a problem as well. Thinking over what you have just done diverts your attention from what is happening now. On the other hand, if you have the time to look over a turn just after you've finished it, it is still fresh in your mind.

8. Turns don't really have an **entry, middle** or an **exit**. Those parts of a turn depend on where the rider takes the control actions that are associated with them: **Entry** is the end of braking and steering; **middle** is

holding mid-turn speed and turning radius; **exit** is where the drive begins.

9. The **idea** of being in control of your location means that you know where you are, where you are going, and the route or direction you will travel to get there. Ideally, you would be able to come up to a turn and make one steering change, and have that "line" work perfectly by getting you exactly where you wanted to go. If you don't have the skill to make that happen, you'll need to make steering changes along the way.

10. In any turn, you are where you are because of what you did with the bike. The decisions you made to get there are based on your **idea** of where you took control actions. Where you did those things is based on your understanding of your location and what that part of the track means to you. In other words, **location is a thought process.**

11. Spending time figuring out your location on the track won't make more work for you. It's intended to free your **attention** so you can work on the other parts of riding. Figuring out a turn is something that can be accomplished and set aside, not an ongoing process to be done each and every lap. You get it set, then go onto traction, speed and the rest, spending as little attention on location as possible.

12. Riders generally only consider their **line** or **direction** in a turn, and pay less attention to current location and future location than they should.

13. The Line Machine is a description of what you do while riding turns, as well as all of the things that are needed to improve your riding. A real machine doesn't yet exist to show you all of the factors of **location**, but you can see that all of its functions are performed by you anyhow. The machine, isn't needed. Sharpening your skills will produce the same ideal for you.

14. Your **location** is the basic building block, the keystone, around which you can work out a **plan** or style of riding. Even though you might be able to ignore one of the other **riding senses** in favor of another, such as paying little attention to **speed** and a great deal to **traction**, you could still get around a turn pretty fast. But, not knowing where you are will undermine all of the other senses.

15. Another way to look at control is from the view that a **line** is the result of what was done to the bike. Compare that idea with its opposite: What was done to the bike is the result of where you wanted to be on the track. Even though you might use both of these methods while learning and experimenting, the second one is how you want to be riding a turn. By having a **future location** figured out, you are leading the bike, not being lead by it.

16. A good idea of your **current location** is important because it is where you are operating the controls to accomplish your **future location**.

17. In combination, current location and future location give you the basis for figuring out **line** or **direction**. A rear-wheel slide changes the direction of the bike; it changes the line.

18. If you have developed sliding as a part of your **plan**, you must slide the bike to make the plan work or you'll have to make a change and run a different line.

19. Understanding the results of the slide puts the rider in control of the situation. If he knows the line has changed and can recalculate the turn, he can make time.

20. Wheelspin coming off a turn does two things: Propels the bike faster and brings the back of the bike around. The result is a faster exit and more room to use the additional speed. When the bike "comes around," it basically widens the turn so you can use the extra speed. Losing the front end will work against the desired effect of sliding the rear end. Getting the bike too sideways anywhere in a turn will lose time.

21. In shooting, the holes produced in the target give the shooter his line. In riding, the rider must use **reference points** or **location** to decide how to ride a turn. He must find things on the track surface to locate himself and accurately cue him as to what to do.

22. Practice your **accuracy** with a goal of being no more than a few inches off your reference points each lap. When you are accurate, you can begin to ride a track, any track, aggressively. At that point, your riding will begin to be tight, positive and certain.

23. Locations problems can be sorted out by breaking the track down into individual turns and practicing each as a separate problem of riding. The technique works very well, and doing it as a drill will make it faster and easier. (The drill is listed in the text.)

Location Questions

All the questions are real close but they are all real different at the same time. One might apply when another one won't.

1. What turns do you feel you don't know well enough?
2. What part of that turn is unclear?
   a) The **approach** (the track leading to it)?
   b) The **entrance** (steering/end of braking)?
   c) The **middle** (little or no change in control)?
   d) The **exit** (where the drive begins)?
3. Is it the basic layout of the turn you don't understand?
4. Are you having trouble doing something in this turn?
   a) Can't get the bike turned where you want to?
   b) Can't get the gas on where you want it?
   c) Too much speed at some point in the turn?
5. Are you waiting for something to happen in the turn, then finding it is too late?
   a) Waiting to roll on the gas for the exit?
   b) Waiting to be able to straighten up the bike?
   c) Waiting for the speed to be right going in?
   d) Waiting for the right place to turn?
6. Do you have **reference points** in the turn that tell you when to perform the actions listed in #5?
7. If you don't have some kind of point to signal you when you perform an action, what is letting you know it's time to do them?
8. Did you ride a turn "right" once and can't do it again?
9. Can you list all the things you pay **attention** to in this turn?
10. What would happen if you had exact points on the track for each of the things you are doing in this turn?

a) Would it help to make your **control timing** better?
b) What is your reason for not having exact reference points on the track?
c) Can you ride the turn "right" without **reference points**?

CHAPTER VI

Timing

It's Not What You Do, But Where You Do It That Counts.

Timing is a big part of it because everyone is doing the same things. It is how you put them together that counts.

Where the control actions are done is all that separates the best riders from the worst.

Look at riding from the perspective of **timing**. Everyone who goes down the road or around a track does virtually the same things to the motorcycle. The throttle goes on and off, the bike is steered into a turn, gears are changed up and down, and so forth. Freddie Spencer has to do all those things, too, you know. Just like we do. The only real difference is **where** they are done on the track.

You don't believe me, right? Let's look at it, and see if it's true or not. You and Freddie come down the front straight on your works bikes. Turn 1 is coming up fast. You roll off the throttle. Freddie waits until he reaches a spot farther down the track to roll it off. The difference is **where**.

You pull on the brakes; he waits and pulls them on down the track a ways. You approach a turn and decide to steer in; he waits and turns later, a little deeper into the turn. He gets on the gas as soon as he's through turning; you wait a little bit, to "get the feel" of things first. He begins his drive out somewhere in the middle of the turn; you do it later.

A plan can be devised by thinking out each action and where you will do it. TIMING.

You see? **Where** the controls are applied is the difference. It's true, he's riding "faster," but think about this: When you exit that turn and get onto the next straightaway, you've both got the gas all the way open; he just gets it wide open sooner than you do. That's **where** it is on the track.

You can nitpick this subject all day long, arguing about degrees of lean angle and all sorts of things, but when you come down to it, **where** the rider does what he does makes the big difference. That's **timing** — **where the rider matches his control operations** (what he does to the bike) **to the track and its changes:** Slow turns, banked turns, off-camber turns, camber changes, bumps, ripples and anything else the track has to offer.

Are you convinced yet that you could be a World Champion?

World-class riders have to have developed **timing** to a precise level of control. Even with changing track situations such as lapping traffic, they're able to adapt that control of their bikes to the necessary changes in line and speed — and almost anything else that comes along — and still go plenty fast.

Timing: Thought Or Motion?

While **timing** is definitely also a **thought process** (because you must know where you want to execute each of the control operations), it is simpler to describe as **motion**. Looking at timing as motion makes it somewhat easier for most riders to grasp.

Timing = the idea that you can, should or will DO SOMETHING when a certain set of track conditions are present.

That notion is nothing fancy. It just means that either from experience or from some other **idea**, you know that you should brake at the end of a 150-mph straight for a 50-mph turn. You know that when the engine revs to redline, you shift. You know that it's good to match the engine rpm with the road speed when you downshift. You know you have to be easy on the throttle when you're in the middle of a slow turn. There are lots of examples.

Timing Breakdown

Timing has two subdivisions; both are important:
1. What you can do **now**.
2. What you **will be able** to do.

While you're out on the track, you'll find yourself frequently switching back and forth between these two things. If you recognize this procedure as **sampling**, you're right. But, it's sampling with a twist, and it's complicated.

Example: Put yourself in the middle of a medium-speed turn, leaned over most of the way, with the throttle on. You're trying to tell from the bike and what it's doing whether you can begin the drive off the turn. A common situation, right? You are trying to **sense** when you can begin that drive.

You're trying to make several decisions at the same time, which is what makes this process so complicated. You are looking at the **timing** of the throttle changes based on what you can do with the throttle **now** and what you **will be able** to do with it in the next segment of time. You're going back over what you've done in the past in this turn, and you're trying to judge how much these current changes are going to affect an outcome you've experienced before. It's a difficult process.

You might think that this is just riding, and you do it all the time. True enough. The question is, how well do you do it? Do you begin that drive 3/10ths of a second later than Freddie Spencer (not much of a hesitation), or do you begin it too soon and have to roll off a little on the exit? It's all a question of **timing**.

If you get in too slow you grab too much throttle and slide.

Smooooth

A really good rider can tell whether a little more throttle right now will change or affect him in the next part of the track coming up. That's a good description of what people call "smooth" on a racetrack. If a rider is smooth, he can time his throttle action so it starts at exactly the right place, allowing him to continue to roll on the throttle all the way through the turn. That smoothness is a direct result of good **timing**.

Time for the drive? NO, NO, NO, maybe, just a little, little more, OK.

66

A Little = A Lot

The timing of each control action on the motorcycle is critical for a good lap time.

Each time you work any of the bike's controls, it's going to make a big difference in how you get around the turn you're in. It should be easy to see that some actions are more critical than others. In the above example, your lap will increase at least that 3/10ths of a second because you didn't get the gas on as soon as the better rider and that will translate into less speed and more time to get to the end of the next straight. On the other hand, it's not as important where you upshift once you're on the straight, as long as you aren't overrevving the engine. But like most things that happen on a racetrack, it's still important.

Time vs. Timing

You have a sense of time and a sense of timing.

These two things are very different, and shouldn't be confused. Your own **sense** of **time** is your personal clock. You can count to yourself, and come close to judging a minute, 10 seconds or whatever. Your sense of time either agrees with a stopwatch, or it doesn't. Trying to judge what to do on a racetrack by this personal clock can be hazardous to lap times — and possibly to your health.

Just as a trick sometimes in practice I get to the place where I think I have to turn and then just wait or count. It's only maybe 1/10th of a second but it works to not get sucked into turning too soon.

Timed Mistakes

All too often, I've heard riders say they can come up to a marker on the track and count to three before they use the brakes. Or else, there's the classic: "I just waited until he braked for the turn, then I counted to three before I put on the brakes and passed him." Get serious. When we talk about racing, we're discussing tenths and hundredths of a second. Your personal clock, under the strain of racing, is about as accurate as a Rolex watch adjusted with an air wrench! Forget it. **Your sense of time is good for telling you when it's time for lunch, not for dictating how you race motorcycles.**

As an example, let's say you're riding a track where there's a short straight followed by a fast turn. You don't have to use the brakes to enter the turn, but you "do" have to roll off the throttle a little on the entrance. You come along the straight, and you've got a point on the track where you begin to lean the bike to enter the turn. Somewhere between the point at which you turn and when you're actually in the turn, you're going to roll off the throttle. When you roll it off will determine how fast you enter the turn. There are two ways of doing this:

1. After you turn at your marker, you hold the gas on for a specified length of time, as determined by your **personal clock.**

2. When you look at the track, **you determine where to roll off the throttle by using your sense of speed, sense of traction, sense of timing and your location on the track.**

Time Warp

Using method #1 is trouble, because you have to put your **attention** on the throttle to get the **timing** right. You've got your attention on your internal clock and your hand on the throttle. Your attention shouldn't be on the controls at this critical stage of the turn, and your ability to judge the time correctly is not going to cut it. Your attention has got to be on the track ahead of you, so you'll have enough information on **where** and **how much** you should roll off the throttle. Your ability to count the tenths of seconds needed to get the throttle action right is greatly diminished by the possibility of going into a 100-mph sweeper too fast! Your ability to count off the seconds becomes warped by the **speed** and other **motions** the bike is making, and will easily change from lap to lap, making your personal clock — and any riding judgments you make based on it — highly inaccurate.

If your attention is "stuck" on the controls, it isn't on the track or the motion of the bike.

Timing Balance

It's fairly simple. You let your **senses** — speed, traction, lean angle and location — determine **where** you do **what** on the track, not the control action itself. If you were to portion it out, you'd spend maybe $8.50 of your **attention** on sensing your track situation, and the remaining $1.50 on the control operations. If the controls cost you less than that, it would be even better.

The thing to remember is that there's a **balance** to how much attention you spend on gathering information, and how much you spend on the controls. That balance should always be weighted heavily toward the information side under all track situations. If you can look over your riding in some turn and recall that your attention was stuck on your control operations, I guarantee you are losing time there.

Sometimes in practice I look at the tach and see where I am in the power then I try and judge the tire slippage at that RPM to see how the bike will react to throttle changes.

Control Solution

Becoming familiar with the controls and how they should be operated in each turn situation is a basic skill.

The above ideal of spending almost nothing on the controls is not easy to accomplish. While you're figuring out some section of the track, you'll have to spend more attention on those control actions than you will later on. It will probably make you feel a little like you are just learning how to ride. Some riders display a problem on this point. They aren't willing to take the time to go through control sequences when they come to a new track or are having trouble with a track they think they know. They believe they "already know how to ride," and that paying **attention** to the basics of **timing** is just for beginners. But think it over. Remember when you and the World Champion were riding on the same track and the same bikes? The real difference was **where** you both used the controls!

In slick turns or off camber it seems the timing takes a lot of thought because you want to slow it down, get it turned and go fast on the drive but you know you can't.

Concentrating your attention on the controls in the first few practice sessions will get it out of the way. Then you can concentrate your attention on riding.

I look at the tach on the exit to see how it worked out gearing wise during practice. If I try something and pick up 1 or 2 hundred RPM, it's good.

Going back to your TIMING basics can help.

Chapter Recap

1. Looking at riding from the point of view of **timing**, you can easily see the main difference in your riding and the world champion's is **where** the control actions are performed.

2. **Timing** is both Thought and Motion but it is primarily Motion. You do something to the bike at an exact place on the track.

3. Not only are you using the Sampling procedure in Timing, but also, you are trying to fit past decisions and experience into the picture as well.

4. Smoothness and good **timing** are one in the same thing.

5. Time and Timing are two very different things. Using your sense of time is good for very little while racing.

6. It may very well be necessary to back off on your speed so you can get your control operations timed just right for a turn.

Questions and Drills

1. Take your favorite track and draw a map of it.
   a. Put a mark on the drawing for each thing you do to the bike: turn, brake, shift, gas on, gas for downshifts, every throttle change you make.
2. Which of these control actions stick in your mind?
   a. Do you have a clear picture of them because you are unsure and spend a lot of **attention** on them?
   b. Do you have a clear picture because you do it very well?
3. If you are hesitating on something: Waiting to downshift, waiting to brake, waiting to turn the throttle on, etc, then:
   a. What is your attention on while waiting?
   b. Did you ever take the time to figure out what you should be doing here?
   c. Are you waiting to change speed or direction?
   d. Did you rush the control actions you were doing just before this?
   e. Did your attention remain on the earlier control action?

Examples:

1. You made a steering change and you're still holding the bars tightly.
2. Coming into the turn, your attention stayed on the brakes or steering and you didn't get the gas on where needed.
3. You made one or more downshifts and you were still listening to the engine.
4. If you are going faster than before:
   a. Have you adjusted your timing of the control actions so they start earlier?
5. You are getting in the turn with more speed but you are waiting the same amount of time as before to turn on the gas.
6. You decided to go in deeper but didn't make the steering procedure quicker. (If you go in deeper, you must steer quicker).
7. If you are going slower than before:
   a. Does it seem that your timing is off everywhere?
   b. Are you waiting in some places and rushed in others?
8. If your riding seems totally "off":
   a. Take a lap at a slower speed and just get your control timing very, very accurate.
   b. Take a fast lap and see if it helped.
   c. Repeat #a until you get it right!

NOTES

CHAPTER VII

Traction

How To Stay Stuck To Planet Earth.

Traction you have now and traction you will have. Seem familiar?

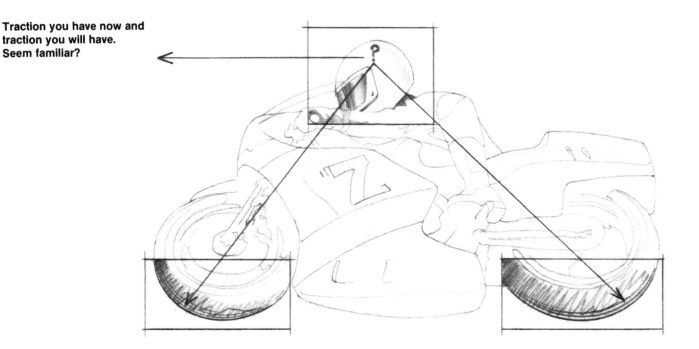

Everybody thinks about traction but the good guys do it more.

Whether you're aware of it or not, traction occupies your thoughts and senses most of the time you're riding.

Let's face it, the only reason you won't go faster is because your bike might slide out. You could, of course, run off the road, but that becomes a traction problem as well. Leaning the bike over too far also ultimately results in a lack of traction.

Traction problems can be broken down into two main areas:

1. **Currently available traction** (What is happening now?)

2. **Future traction** (Will what I'm doing now result in traction or no traction later on?)

Sense Of Traction

Traction is a combination of **thought** and **motion**. You take what you are sensing (motion), and match it to your **idea** of how well the bike should or can stick (thought). You **sample** the traction. If your **idea** of traction matches the real traction that is available, you are right; if you think the bike will stick better than it can, you are wrong. Underrating traction is also "wrong."

Example: When you set the speed of the bike before you enter a turn, your main concern is whether or not the bike will still stick at that speed when it's leaned over. You are looking at your **idea** of how fast the bike can go and still stick, while leaned over. That is a question of **future traction**.

Once you are in the turn, as you work the throttle, your attention is on **available traction**. As you begin to drive out of the turn, you're again considering **future traction**, but you keep track of the **available traction** as well.

Traction Judge

At almost every place on the track, you have to concern yourself with **available traction** as well as **future traction**. You can **sample** your available traction. You must **judge** future traction. And judging future traction is a complicated process. As an example, consider what you do while just entering most turns:

1. You **sample** the current speed.
2. You **judge** how it compares with previous runs.
3. You decide how that matches up with your **idea** of the "right" speed.
4. You begin adjusting the speed to match your **idea**.
5. You **project** that speed into the turn.
6. You decide whether there will be traction at that projected speed. It's a decision about **future traction** because you aren't there yet.
7. You make any final **speed** adjustments that are required.
8. You again **sample** the traction just after you turn.
9. You **judge** (sample) the speed, right or wrong, at the point when you are through steering and the bike is leaned over and stable, against your **idea** of **traction**.
10. You **decide** to correct the speed or leave it as it is.

Those 10 steps don't even touch on steering, the use of brakes, or any of the steps of locating where you are on the track. Now, are you busy or what?

Sense Of Speed

Sense of speed = your ability to judge whether you are riding faster or slower than you were during previous runs through a given section.

Your **sense of speed** and your ability to repeat a speed on any part of a track is an integral part of successful racing. If you can't remember how fast you were going the last time around a turn, you can't predict how well your bike will stick.

You really do have to have a good sense of traction in the rain because you come around the next lap and you don't know whether it rained more or not.

Decisions about your riding usually are balanced by your SENSE and IDEA of TRACTION.

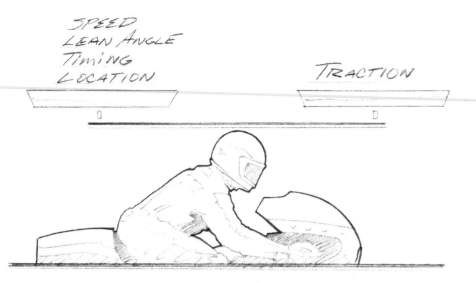

SPEED
LEAN ANGLE
TIMING
LOCATION   TRACTION

The ability to predict **future traction** is a **thought** process. The ability to sense speed is a combination of **senses** and **speed memory**. You remember how fast you went before, then judge your current speed against it. That's **sampling** again. You switch your attention back and forth, from the **motion** back to the **thought**, to keep a running report on how things are going.

Note: More on sense of speed in Chapter VIII, "Braking."

Traction Or Speed?

You can predict traction only as well as you can sense speed.

If your **sense of speed** isn't well developed, your **traction prediction** won't be either. If you're in a turn trying to figure out whether you're riding faster or slower than the last time through, you aren't predicting traction — far from it. You're adjusting the speed, but you aren't sure what to adjust it to. You have no **target speed** in mind.

You know how fast you want to go and what felt comfortable. It would be hard to just concentrate on speed, you might miss your turn points or traction limit.

Does your sense of speed tell you how fast to go, or is it your sense of traction? Does knowing the track and pavement allow you to predict traction? Does having a **plan** allow you to judge both **speed** and **traction**, or is it all the above?

Adjusting Speed

On most tracks, at competitive speeds, 1 second in improvement is equal to a 1-mph-faster average lap. It means that your **sense of speed** must be

The actual mph isn't important but your sense of speed is.

79.5

really accurate. It means you need to be sensitive down to fractions of a mph. It means, ultimately, that your improvement depends on how well you can judge speed. If you are going to ride with control, you've got to have the ability to **sense speed**.

Not only are a good **sense of speed** and a good **speed memory** necessary to improvement, they are also the best insurance a rider can have.

Let's say that your **sense of speed** was accurate to within 1/100th mph. You could go around a track and just increase your speed by 1/100th mph each time you entered, went through the middle and made your drive off the turns.

Provided the tires didn't change very much and the suspension continued to work, not only would you eventually be able to make the maximum speed through the turns, you would also have very little chance of falling — at least not from excess speed, a common cause of "get-offs." If your **sense of speed** was this precise, you'd still be able to make speed increases past the point where the bike began to slide!

It seems obvious that a top rider must have a **sense of speed** developed to within ¼ to ½ mph. And the top riders do. Otherwise, they couldn't cut laps consistent to within 2/10ths of a second.

The same applies to you. If you want to pick up ½ of a second on a racetrack, you only have to go ½-mph-faster average for 1 lap. When you can do that, **traction** is a much simpler subject. In fact, **your confidence as a rider is only as good as your ability to judge speed**, because speed is the most important part of traction.

Look over your own riding and see if this isn't true.

Traction Distraction

Increasing the speed of your bike in any turn creates an unknown **future traction** situation. As you run through the turn, you must **project** your new, faster speed and traction situation ahead.

Increased speed is only one distraction. Gear changes while leaned over, as well as bumps, ripples, and changes in pavement or camber, all can cause **future traction** problems.

You must decide how much attention you will spend on traction. If you devote too much attention to this one aspect of riding, you can become lost on the track. Now, that might sound odd, but it's fairly common, especially with new riders. You can watch them go around a turn while rolling the throttle on and off. If they're overly concerned with cornering clearance, another element that affects traction, the bike might be at five or six lean angles through one section. Or, the rider might feel good with the speed/traction/lean angle that he has at the moment, but he's unable to **project** it into a future part of the turn.

Traction vs. Speed

Your ability to predict future traction monitors your speed.

You will only go as fast as you think you can. Those are your **thoughts** on how much **motion** (speed) you can make. The amount of **traction**

The entrance is the most important part of the traction problem. Speeds are high and brakes are on some. After you get in, you can unweight the nose some and ride it.

Changing the speed in a turn to get it back up after a mistake is hard because of the extra acceleration. It is hard to judge future traction.

75

you believe you will have in the next instant will, to a great extent, determine your speed.

Present-Future?

Most riders use a sense of current traction to try to predict future traction.
Examples:
1. **Currently available traction:** "The bike is sliding now," or, "The bike is at the limit of traction."
2. **Future traction:** "Will it quit sliding? or, "Will it stay at the limit?" or, "Will it go over the limit?"

Does this seem familiar? Just as tomorrow is difficult to predict, so is **future traction**. The rider who doesn't know the track and all its changes is always "stuck" with his attention on **currently available traction**, and he tries to read the future from it.

When you don't know what is going to happen with future traction you have to be willing to take chances to see what happens.

It's true that this rider "might" have a better chance of staying upright if he rode over a slippery section (oil or gas on the track) if he already had all of his attention focused on **available traction**, but he wouldn't be the faster rider on the track.

Traction Basic

You can use more lean angle on the 250.

The farther you lean the bike, the less acceleration you can use.
Most riders understand this. The tires will take only so much cornering force before they slide. If you have the bike leaned over all the way,

At these lean angles traction is at its lowest point.

then try to accelerate hard, the tires won't take it. As you begin to straighten the bike up, the acceleration factor can be greater because cornering load is lessened.

Crest Traction

When you go around a turn that has a crest, the bike will become light as it goes over, reducing **available traction**. The load on the tires is reduced, producing a smaller contact patch, but the cornering forces haven't changed. Accelerating compounds the problem by making the bike even lighter, creating a pronounced tendency to wheelie.

You can carry the speed you have when you reach the crest over the crest.

Obviously, this depends on how steep the crest is. If it is steep, you have to roll back the throttle to hold an even speed or very slight acceleration. As soon as the bike "lands" and compresses the suspension again, you can increase acceleration.

Bumps And Banks

A banked turn is just the reverse of a crest. You can accelerate through the banked part of a turn. As the banking flattens out, you have to raise the bike up to begin your drive. If your chosen line has the bike still leaned over all the way when you exit a banked turn, you won't be able to accelerate hard.

Some bumps and dips can increase traction.

Some bumps can be used just like a berm. Actually, a bump/dip is like a crested turn and a banked one at the same time. If you accelerate over them, you'll have the same traction considerations as if you were riding over a crest. If you go over bumps with even throttle and wait until the bike "lands," you can accelerate by taking advantage of the loaded tires and suspension. It's all in the timing of the throttle whether you get traction or lose it going over them.

By knowing where the bumps and banks are, you can predict future traction.

It should be clear that the rider who can use every last foot of banked track to his advantage will be faster than someone who can't — a "lot" faster. You could race with someone who didn't lean his bike over as far as you did, who wasn't willing to slide, who didn't get terrific drives off turns, and he still could beat you because he used the banking better than you did. Even a slightly banked turn is a big advantage when used properly.

Some bumps or ripples help you get the bike turned because it's like braking the tire loose a little.

Dirt Tracker's Traction

An important part of dirt track racing is finding the **traction**. Finding it means control, because acceleration is only possible when you've got **traction**. Dirt track riders know this and apply it to road racing. Many people have said that dirt trackers make good road racers because they

The "feet up" slide. Can this rider predict future traction?

This is serious traction.

are used to sliding. But, what are these guys doing? They're just finding where the traction is.

Dirt Tracker's "Line"

Sometimes you can have too much traction and it makes it hard to turn the bike.

A "line" to dirt trackers means; Where is the traction? If the traction is low in the turn, they go low. If it's high, the best line is the high line. These guys look at a turn from the viewpoint of **traction**. To them, a "line" is just a handy way to get to that **traction**.

The dirt track world has devised a language of terminology to deal with **traction**. Each different traction situation can define a different **plan** of riding. A "groove track,"* a "blue groove,"* "tacky,"* "cushion"* and "slick,"* among others, are all terms for traction and the quality of traction.

*Glossary

78

Traction Training

As if the job of dirt racing weren't difficult enough already, there is the added dimension of changing track conditions. The flat tracker might find vast differences in **traction** from practice to the heat races, and then from the heats to the main event. Even during the course of a race, riders sometimes have to "chase" the traction. If, for instance, a track begins to dry out on the inside, riders might have to follow the wetter earth (which has better traction) to the outside as the race progresses. Wherever the traction is, that's the best line.

A line is only as good as the traction is offers.
No matter how perfect your **plan** is, or how pretty your line is, you've got to get the bike to stick the best way possible. The good part of road racing is that once you find the **traction**, it usually doesn't change much during the course of the day, at least, not on it's own. Once you've found the **traction**, you can begin to work on the fine points of adjusting your **plan** to take advantage of it.

Predicting Traction

Even someone with a very good **sense of traction** will be at a disadvantage if he doesn't know where to use it. The rider who has all of his attention on the **available traction** will always be too late to take advantage of it.

When you go into a banked turn and begin to feel the traction advantage, you're already too late to use it.
You have to be ready and accelerating before you ever get to the banking. Here again, you have the situation in which the rider finds that he could be going faster, but he cannot reach that faster speed because the acceleration would be too severe for the tires and the suspension. He might find himself going in 2 mph too slow, but turning on the gas hard enough to achieve that extra 2 mph would cause the bike to slide out. Another rider, who knew he could be riding 2 mph faster in that same corner doesn't have to accelerate. He can keep his attention on what he's doing, and concentrate on his immediate problems. Rider No.1 is trying to make up for a mistake that rider No. 2 never made.

Flat turns, or even off-camber turns, are much the same as banked ones in this respect. The rider must be able to **predict** his traction to go into them at the highest possible speed.

Traction/Suspension/Stability

The reason your bike was designed the way it was — everything from the frame to the fork, shocks, steering geometry, even the wheelbase — was to maximize traction.
You could say that the bike's suspension was a major limiting factor. While that's true, bear in mind that the whole purpose of the suspension is to maintain traction during speed changes and steering procedures. It's all there to help keep both wheels in as even and predictable a trac-

If you don't spin the tires you get a lot of frame flex and that can get you when it unflexes.

tion situation as possible.

Stability is an important part of the traction equation, but, ultimately, **stability is traction**. If a bike wiggles around, it produces an intermittent traction condition. The wiggling or bobbing up and down causes the tires to load and unload, changing traction. You can't keep the gas on if the back end is going from side to side and up and down at the same time, even on the straights.

Suspension Mystery

Suspension is a big mystery to most riders. But it becomes much simpler when you look at it from the point of view of **traction**.

You don't have handling problems; you have traction problems. Bad handling = poor traction. And, poor traction = bad handling.

No matter how you slice it up, you're just trying to keep the two factors of motion under control, and **traction is the limiting factor for speed and steering changes**. It might not be much comfort, but you can think of a tank-slapper as an extreme traction problem!

Suspension Tuning

From a practical viewpoint, you tune the suspension to help you gain traction where you need it. Raising and lowering the front or rear of the bike transfers weight from one end of the bike to the other affecting traction. Stiffening the fork springs or shock springs affects how the bike reacts to the road. Compression and rebound damping rates do the same. Fork/swingarm/frame rigidity affect how much leverage you can apply to the bike before it becomes a spring itself. If the frame is weak, the bike displays a residual reaction to pavement changes and cornering loads. The frame "stores up" the load with stress, like a spring, then returns it when it is unloaded. This spring effect changes traction. A weak fork acts in the same way to affect traction, as does a flexible swingarm.

The rider must figure out where on the track he is having suspension-traction problems. That section has some pavement variations such as bumps or ripples or whatever.

The problem can occur going into a turn, in the middle of the turn or at the exit. Going in, the weight usually is more on the front end of the bike. In the middle, it is more of an even transfer. At the exit, more weight is transfered to the rear from acceleration. A problem at any of those points probably has something to do with weight transfer. You begin by adjusting the end that is loaded.

If one end of the bike is stiffer than the other, it can transfer the load, making the bike handle poorly. (Ideally, the front would handle what came its way, and the back would handle its own problems separately.) It's usually better to set the bike up to allow the rear to handle the problems rather than the front, because the front end is attached to the bike by the steering head, which rotates. The rear end is held to the chassis by the swingarm. Failure on the part of the front end to handle its suspension problems can result in a tank-slapper. The idea is more readily observable in dirt bikes. A good off-road rider will try to wheelie over rough spots as often as possible, which forces the rear suspension to deal with the suspension loads. That's not always possible on a road bike, and too light a front end can be a problem as well.

If you skid the front, sometimes you can climb up on the high side of the bike and change the weight so it doesn't slide out.

The suspension acts to stabilize traction. The bike is smooth when it's working.

The goal here isn't to solve your suspension problems, but to point out where you should begin to look for the cure. And most important, that you should look for it from the ultimate purpose of the suspension: **traction**.

Note: If you have a GP bike with many suspension adjustments, you usually can find tires that work well for a given track; then begin to dial-in your suspension. If you are racing a production bike, you are more limited in terms of the suspension changes that can be made, and you might find it easier to fit the tires to the suspension rather than the other way around. Most street bikes are sensitive to tire construction. Oftentimes, one tire is vastly better than another either in steering or in adhesion. If you can find a tire that does both well, you are in business.

Traction Checklist

Use this checklist on every turn where traction is a problem, or use it to see if traction was the problem.

1. Was your attention stuck on **traction** someplace in this turn?
   a) On the entry?
   b) In the middle?
   c) At the exit?
   d) Someplace else?
2. Was your attention stuck on your **currently available traction**?
   Was your attention stuck on **future traction?**
3. **Was that traction** problem:
   a) Too much speed?
   b) Too much lean angle?
   c) Pavement problems?
      1) Ripples?
      2) A bump?
      3) A dip?
      4) An asphalt seam?
      5) An asphalt patch?
   d) At a steering change?
   e) At a speed change?
      1) Accelerating?
      2) Decelerating?
   f) Pavement appears slippery
   g) Pavement looks "tacky" and isn't?
   h) Problem with tires?
   i) Problem with suspension?
   j) Are you holding the bike too tightly?
   k) Are there camber changes?
4. If bike lost traction, did you:
   a) Think there would be traction and there wasn't?
   b) Try a line you never tried before?
   c) Did you decide to take a corner at a faster speed?
5. Do you have some other thoughts about this part of the track?
   a) Did you fall here before?
   b) Did you almost fall here before?
   c) Did you see or hear about someone falling here before?
   d) Some other thoughts?

NOTES

CHAPTER VIII

Braking

Less May Be More And More Is Usually Less.

Ultra hard braking can distract you from other things.

It's hard to comment on a lot of these chapters because it's all there and I don't have anything to add.

The brakes cause more problems for riders than any other control.

The front brake on a motorcycle is the most powerful control on the machine by a factor of at least two. No matter how fast your bike is, or how much horsepower it's got, you can probably stop it twice as fast as it will accelerate! Your bike might do 120 mph in the quarter-mile, but you'd better hope it will stop in a lot less than that. And it will.

The engine is essentially a gasoline processor. It turns gasoline into heat and, in the course of that processing, the fuel expands. How it expands, and how well the power it generates is transmitted through all the gears and chains to the rear wheel determines how much power the bike will have.

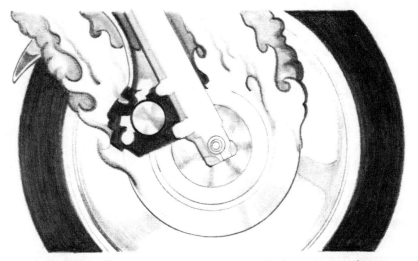

The brakes reverse that entire procedure. **Brakes are motion processors: They turn motion into heat.** How well they do it determines how well your brakes work. If, for instance, the brake pads are too hard, they won't generate enough heat from friction and the bike won't stop well. Using pads with too much friction, pads that are too soft, will generate more heat than the system can handle. The pads will wear out quickly, and the discs can't get rid of the heat quickly enough to perform well.

Brakes are an adjustment. We use them to adjust the speed of the bike, downward, to match an **idea** of how fast the bike should be going. What is more important, having great brakes or having a good idea of how fast you want to be going in a turn? Which will improve your lap times the most?

Speed Ideas

Take a close look at your **idea** of speed. As you approach the turn at the end of a straight, one of your top priorities is to reduce the speed so you can enter the turn. Reduce to what? Down to your **idea** of how fast the turn can be entered. You're going to do battle with this turn, and you have two weapons: The brake lever and your **idea** of how fast to enter it. That's all you've got. If you want to call the idea judgment, that's fine. If you want to call it a feeling, that's OK, too. It doesn't matter what you call it; it's the result of your **thoughts** on how fast to go.

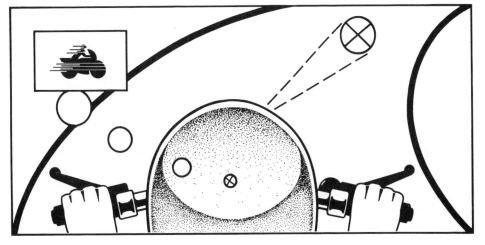

Your Idea of how fast to go monitors your speed.

85

You can look back to the primitive viewpoint most people have about racing, and say experience is the only thing that tells you how fast to go. What's experience? You notice something and you record it. If you can learn from experience, it means you figured something out and can use that experience again to your advantage. OK, you entered the turn and

OK, you entered the turn and noticed you could've taken it faster (**thought**). The next lap, you hold the **idea** of how fast you went, then you increased the speed to match the **new idea** of how fast it can be done. That same process holds true for the middle and the exit of the turn, as well.

Sense Of Speed

Your sense of speed determines how well you can adjust your idea of speed.

Finding yourself going too slow entering a turn is based on the thought that you had more traction left. You make part of your decision to go faster by that thought.

You had a thought: "I can do it a little faster." That's an easy thought to have. Now, as you approach the same turn again, the big question is: **How much** faster? Right then, as you are making the final adjustments (braking) in the bike's speed to enter the turn, your life is in the hands of your **sense of speed**. If a little faster means 3/10ths mph, you're in good shape. If it means 3 mph, you're going to scare yourself! **To increase or decrease speed, you rely on your sense of speed.**

Speed information comes in and you weigh it against your Idea of speed for that section, then adjust it.

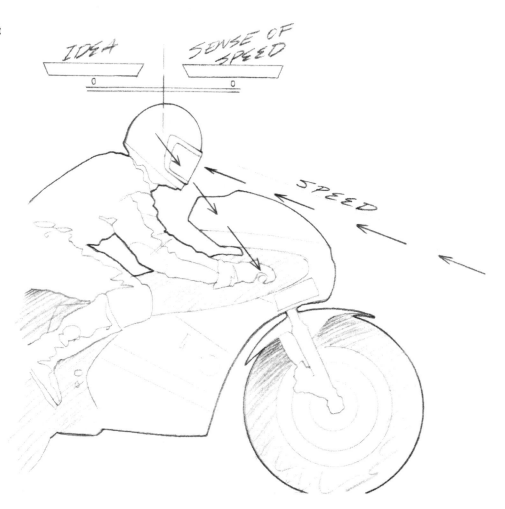

Speed Memory/Sense Of Speed

Speed memory and sense of speed are very different. If you have a good **speed memory**, you'll be able to get into the turn at the same speed you went the last time. But, your **idea** was to "increase" the speed. If you haven't gone any faster through this turn at some time in the past, you won't be able to rely on your **speed memory** to get the extra speed you want. You have to judge the increase you want with your **sense of speed**.

Speed memory = your ability to recall a speed you have run before.

You might not want to remember a speed you were going just before a crash, but you'll easily remember one you liked, for one reason or another. It felt fast, it felt good, and you could control the bike.

Inspired Speed

Often, a rider will become inspired, and get into a turn faster than he's ever gone before. Maybe he was taking a chance, maybe he was following someone faster than he is. If his **speed memory** is good, he finds out the turn can be run faster than before, and he'll hold that new **idea** of the faster speed. His lap times go down, and he's happy. Has that ever happened to you?

There isn't anything wrong with that, except that you didn't do it on your own. Will you be able to do it again? Maybe . . . and maybe not. Will you be able to apply it to other turns? Perhaps. Will you have to continue pumping your adrenaline to redline to go faster in the turns?

Brakes And Turns

Entering turns where brakes are used involves these three factors:

1. **Speed memory** — how fast you've gone.

2. **Target speed** — your **idea** to go faster or slower (and exactly how much either way).

3. **Sense of speed** — your ability to feel the difference between **speed memory** and **target speed**.

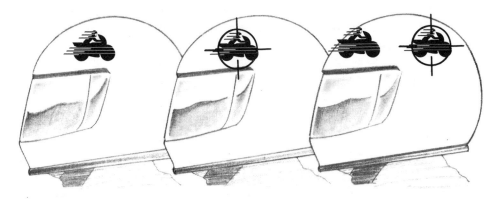

Speed memory: How fast you have gone.

Target speed: How fast you want to go.

Sense of speed: Adjusting your speed to match your target.

Here is the rider again turning **motion** into a **thought**, having an idea, then translating that thought back into motion. In this case, the brakes are used to make it happen.

Most riders are OK on Number 1, **speed memory**. You can verify that by noting consistent trends in their lap times. They might be changing lines and braking points and all kinds of things, but they seem to come up with fairly consistent times; **speed memory** seems to explain it. Is that true for you?

Number 2, an **idea** to go faster or slower, is common to just about everyone. I've never really talked to a rider who didn't have the **idea** that he could go faster at one time or another.

The last of the three factors, adjusting speed, is where most everyone falls short. Time after time I've worked with riders who go out with a tooth-grinding purpose to go faster in one turn, but fail to do it. The rider knows he can do it. The bike isn't sliding and he's in control, but he just can't get the additional speed he wants. If you've ever raced, the same thing has happened to you. Right?

Speed Adjustment Problems

Normal braking might look like this.

Late braking cuts the time and distance you have to get your speed right.

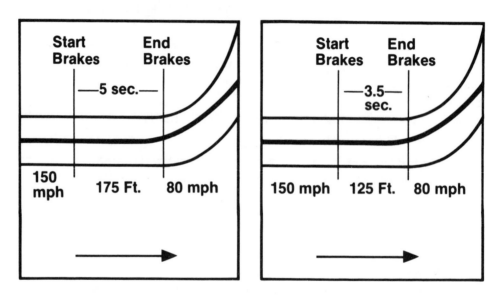

Entering a "braking turn" is a **speed** and **distance** problem. You allow yourself a certain amount of track space to reach your **target speed** to enter the turn. The distance from the place where you begin to brake until the place where you're in the turn is the space you've allotted to do this job. If you brake late, you allow yourself less space — and less time — to adjust your speed to the target speed.

Sampling

The process of **sampling** is also compressed if you brake late. You have to switch your **attention** back and forth to do this. The later you brake, the faster you have to sample your **ideas** and **motion**, and the less time you have to pay attention to each.

In a turn, you sample your **speed memory**, your **target speed** and your **sense of speed**. Speed memory is the baseline speed that you remember. Target speed is what you are trying to get to. Sense of speed is what you use to get there.

Braking Purpose

The purpose of braking is to adjust the speed to match your idea.

You're trying to get the speed right so no further adjustments have to be made once you're in the turn. If you don't get the speed right, you've made a mistake. Chances are that no one will notice it except you, but as you know, that's enough of an audience! When you enter a turn and find yourself going slower than you wanted, a four-step process takes place. The result of the process usually is a frustrated rider:

1. **Thought:** You **notice** that the speed isn't what you wanted (usually not fast enough).

2. **Thought:** You have to judge how much too slow your current speed is. You take the time to **sample** the speed.

3. **Thought:** You are already in the turn, so it's necessary to **recalculate** how much acceleration you can get away with. (These three steps are the time-lag before you turn the throttle.)

4. **Motion:** You begin to make the **adjustment** with the throttle.

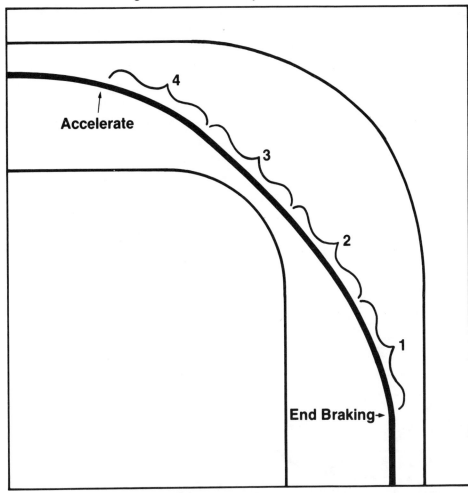

Making a mistake with your speed adjustment is at least a 4 step process. (see text)

The whole reason that this is a mistake is that each of those steps takes some time — and **attention** — and the track is flying by while you think things through. By the time you have it all figured out, the exit is at hand and that's a whole different problem. You've "blown" the turn. Look over your own riding. The reason it takes most of the turn to "correct" for a slow entry speed are the above points.

Foggy Speed

You actually have two factors at work while you are braking:

1. Rate of deceleration. (The braking forces.)
2. The speed as it changes from faster to slower.

Confusing the two can complicate this important action. As you're braking into a turn, the forces are severe. Your body is being driven forward onto the tank, the bike's front end is compressed, and you would actually be thrown off the bike and run over by it if you weren't holding on tightly! The **force of deceleration**, how quickly the bike is slowing, can consume a great deal of your **attention** as a result of those forces. Rightfully so, because those forces are a major source of information for judging your braking traction.

Real Speed

Underlying the force of deceleration is the **actual speed** the bike is travelling. One of the reasons it's hard to judge speed going into a turn is that the speed is often masked by this other powerful force at work. **Judging the speed by the deceleration force is like trying to see where you are when the windshield is fogged.** Complicating the problem is the fact that the speed is changing rapidly, and must be **sampled** regularly if you're to keep track of it. You clean a portion of the windshield, only to have it fog again; you clean another patch, it fogs again. Your **sense of speed** is the thing being fogged or masked by the forces.

It's sometimes nearly impossible to take your **attention** away from the **deceleration factor** long enough to get a good reading on the speed of the bike. The harder the braking, the more difficult it is to take your attention away from it. Using the above example again, while the windshield is clean, you can keep track of the changing scene in front of you.

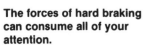

The forces of hard braking can consume all of your attention.

As it fogs again, your attention is drawn to the fog and you begin to lose your place on the road. As the fog closes in, you're forced to try to locate yourself on the road by objects that are closer and closer to the vehicle, until you see nothing but the fog.

The smart car driver turns the defroster on for a while, and clears a "window" in the fog. Most of the fog is still there and he has to make an effort to look through the cleared section, but he can see enough to drive.

As a rider, you have to clean a place in the "fog" created by the **deceleration force**, so that you can view the **speed changes** under braking.

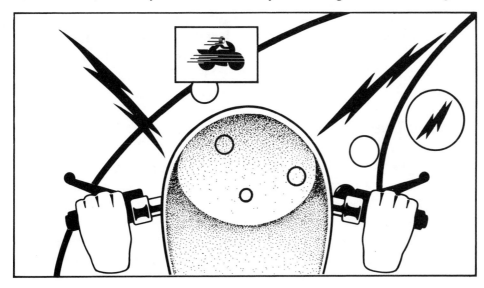

You have to separate the braking forces from speed sensing. They are two different things.

Corrected Entry

If you've gotten your entry speed correct, there's a good chance that the rest of the turn went smoothly. That's most likely because you were able to spend your **attention** on the turn and not on correcting the wrong speed. **When your entry speed is correct, more attention can be spent riding the turn.**

Stumbling Entry

The biggest stumbling block to this is that riders still think they must brake as deeply as possible into each turn. Late braking is something everyone can relate to, and it's a drill that anyone can do. Unfortunately, the late braking requires too much **attention** for most riders and they can't use whatever **sense of speed** they have. The pressure of late braking just doesn't allow them to adjust. So, the late braking turns into a question of survival, not a riding technique. The eyes become very large in these situations, and the attention is focused on the braking, nothing else. Sound familiar?

When I talk about a "correct" entry speed — I mean one "that will make you happy" — probably a little faster than last time with the bike still under control. On a motorcycle, that is happy. A good **sense of speed** will make that possible.

Late braking is hard, you get too much attention on the brakes and forget about turning and speed.

Speed Refinement

You can see that a poor sense of speed will keep you from getting what you want on a racetrack. What would a really good sense of speed get you? Suppose again, that your sense of speed was so good that you could increase or decrease the bike's speed by 1/100ths mph. To you, going a "little faster" would mean 1/100ths mph faster. If your senses were as finely honed as that, you could just continue adjusting your speed until you got it right for that bike, tires, suspension, and riding plan.

You might never get your **sense of speed** to that state of refinement. There is a way to improve your braking, sense of speed and speed memory. It's called the "No-Brakes" Drill. **Just ride without using the brakes**. How will it improve your braking? How will it improve your sense of speed? How will it do anything but scare you? Let's see.

Braking Theory

If we agree that the whole purpose of using the brakes is to adjust the speed of entry into a turn, we've got a starting point. Do you agree? Or, do you believe that there's lots of time to be made up with brakes?

Whether your braking is so-so or really good, the most you could hope to make up on an average track is 2/10ths - 5/10ths of a second, and that would be with teeth-gritting, absolutely heroic braking. If you need more than 2/10ths of a second to win or even beat the guy in front of you, don't look to make it up with the brakes. As every good rider from the past has found, you make time with the throttle on, not off!

On the other hand, if you can see that getting into, through and out of a turn at +1 mph will get you down the next straight 1 mph faster, and you add that to your average speed for the track, you'll also see a much larger difference in your lap times, and you'll get it without hyperextending your eyeballs.

Speed Drill

For this drill, let's say you are coming down a 175-mph straight, going into a 75-mph turn. In this case, 75 mph is the speed you have in mind; it's your **target speed**. Your immediate job is to get the bike adjusted to 75 mph. If you use the brakes to do it, let's say it takes 500 feet. If you don't use the brakes, let's say it takes 1000 feet to adjust your speed. Will it change your **entry speed** if you take that 1000 feet to adjust your speed? Of course not. It will change your lap time overall, but that isn't what you're working on here.

So, the drill is: Ride the track with no brakes.

Brakes don't determine your entry speed. Entry speed is a question of target speed, sense of speed and speed memory.

No matter how good or bad your brakes are, they don't set the speed for a turn; **you do**. You have a **target speed** in mind. You use your **sense of speed** and **speed memory**. The brakes are only a tool to reach your target speed.

Using no brakes makes you rely on your sense of speed and speed memory. That's what you're trying to develop with this drill. Not using the brakes takes away all the distraction the brakes can produce, and it allows you to spend your **attention** on just sensing speed and adjusting it. Once you take away use of the brakes, you can see just how much attention you actually use to get your entry speed correct. Understand?

Tested Theory

The No-Brakes Drill is not an untried theory. At the Advanced School sessions of the California Superbike School, I've run this drill with about 800 students. Those who had run the same track the day before we did had up to a 25-second improvement in lap times while doing this drill!

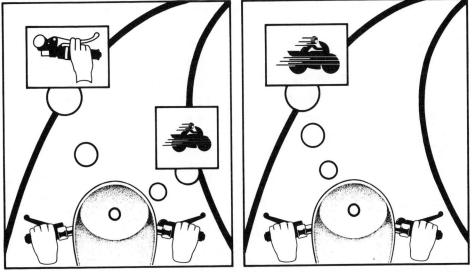

With brakes; a lot of attention is on braking, less is on speed.

Without brakes, all of your attention can be put on sensing speed.

Even riders who were doing well the day before cut up to seven seconds off their lap times.

When really good riders perform this drill, they say they actually can get into turns better without using the brakes. The brakes distract them from spending their **attention** on **sense of speed** and **speed memory**, and the brakes do the same thing to you. Typically, with a good rider, the lap times are about four seconds slower than the best times with the brakes. That's on a track with 3-5 places to brake, such as Willow Springs in California.

The major problem with this drill occurs in open practice. If you're a good rider, people will want to follow you. When you roll off the gas early, someone could easily run into you. So, do this drill when no one is following you.

Brakes/No Brakes

If you can't get the speed set right without the brakes, you have no hope of doing it with them.

Take another look at this drill. If you can't get the speed set right, for you, by using two to three times the space on the track, there's no way you are going to get it when you compress that period of adjustment by using the brakes.

Your **sense of speed** and **speed memory** are developed to a point somewhere between very good and very bad. This drill will separate these two abilities — they are among the most important riding abilities you've got — and will also help you to work with them. Without them, you're just floundering around on the track, hoping to get it right by luck.

Note: If you want to practice hard braking, you can do it on the pit lane or in a parking lot. You don't need to take up valuable track time to learn that lesson. You can even practice it on the street without breaking any speed laws.

Speed Set

Another tremendous benefit of the No-Brakes Drill is that you must put your **attention** on the turn coming up. You will notice, as you do it, that you're able to spend a lot more attention on where you're going to enter the turn. You'll make your major steering change there and actually enter the turn. You'll spend a lot of attention on it, because that is where your speed must be correct. It's also the place you'd be finished with the brakes if you had used them. That would be your **end-of-braking marker** or area.

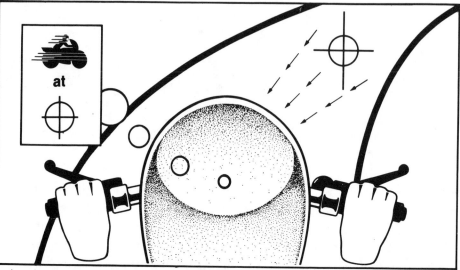

The No Brakes Drill makes it easier to set up turn entry and become more accurate.

In almost every situation, the very best riders in the world finish their braking as they make their steering change while they are leaning the bike over. As maximum lean angle is attained, the brakes are off and the throttle is on again. The amount of throttle used depends on the turn.

As you approach a turn without using the brakes, you'll begin to realize how important that little area is. You'll see that time between when you begin to lean the bike over and when you finish as being very important. **That is the point at which you make or break your turn entry.**

More Lessons

There is another benefit you will get from this drill. You can stop using beginning-brake markers. It's a trap to rely on a beginning-brake marker, as most people do, to gauge your braking. It's easy to get the **idea** from

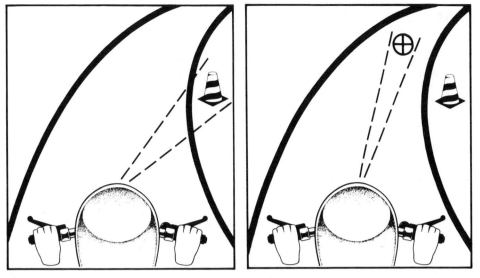

Off track brake markers take your attention away from the track.

Using an End of Braking Marker keeps your attention on the track.

listening to most riders talk that everything will work out OK if you just have a good brake marker. It isn't true. **The important point is where you "end" the braking, not where you begin it!**

Riders at all levels of skill (except the very top) suffer under this **idea** at one time or another. They think that having a brake marker will magically make everything work out right. What really happens is that the rider becomes dependent on these beginning-brake markers, and he doesn't put his **attention** on **sense of speed** and **speed memory**. Riders think they're going to set up this braking procedure so they won't have to pay attention to it. It's a marvelous idea with just one flaw: It won't work.

It won't work because things change. You might come out of the last turn a few mph faster or slower. That will change the beginning marker quite a lot. The brakes will heat up and change during a race. That alters things, too. You just have to learn how to use the brakes properly when entering a turn, there's no substitute. The right way is quite simple. **You look ahead to the end-of-braking marker to judge your beginning-brake point.** When you use the brakes, that's what you must learn to do. You'll be surprised how much simpler the whole job of entering a turn becomes. If you have ever felt "frozen" on the brakes, it's because you didn't have an end-of-braking area. **You had no place to look ahead and adjust your speed to.** Does that still happen sometimes?

Using brake markers is not good, you look at the track. Use a marker to estimate your location but you have to look at the track to keep your speed right.

Some More Parts

Whether you use the brakes or are doing this drill, you're going to require good **depth perception**. That's the other part of this activity. You must judge the distance between where you are and the place you'll be done slowing down. Along with that, you are gauging the whole thing with **sense of speed** and **speed memory**. It's easy to see that poor depth perception would make this process very hard, indeed. Whether your depth perception is good or bad, it won't hurt to have some kind of marker to remind you that it's time to begin thinking about braking — or rolling off the throttle, if you're doing the drill. It's not a brake marker, it's a reminder. You'll do this without anyone telling you, I'm sure.

One More

Once you get good end-of-braking markers (doing the No-Brakes Drill will help), you'll have a lot less trouble passing when going into turns. In fact, **having an end-of-braking marker is the key to passing while braking.** Try it. If you have a good end-of-braking marker, I promise you'll have less trouble passing when entering a turn, provided you look ahead to the marker and not at the rider you're passing.

No Brakes Two Ways

There are two ways to do the **no brakes drill**. Both of them have value. The first and most obvious way is to come down the straight and shut off the gas as late as you think you can and still be able to get the bike into the turn at your **target speed**.

The second way of doing it is to shut off well before the turn so the bike will be going slower than your **target entry speed**. Doing it this second way will help to get your awareness of speed skills developed from lower to higher speeds. If you only practice setting the speed coming down the scale of **mph** you only have ½ of the ability you need to race.

You want to develop your **sense of speed** going up the scale, accelerating, and down the scale, decelerating. You do need both.

Often times race tracks are designed so that the first turn is fairly close to the start/finish line. In some cases the first turn is actually faster than the bikes are going from a standing start. Here is where a rider with a very good **sense of speed** and **speed memory** really pulls out. You have probably seen this happen at the start of a race. One rider is already in race mode while the others look like they are shutting off from habit. They don't have as good a **sense of speed** and **speed memory** as the fast guy. That is something you can immediately apply this drill to.

No Brakes Three Ways

The third dimension you can add to this drill is **not using the engine to slow** you down, not downshifting when you come into the turn. In doing this drill, you're not trying to get into the turn fast, you're trying to get in at the right speed, your **target speed**. Even if you almost stop coming up to a turn, then accelerate up to it, that's OK. As long as your **entry speed** was right, you got it.

Not using the engine to slow you down — which it doesn't do a very good job of anyway — will save you some additional **attention** going into the turn. You won't have to spend anything on using the throttle to match your engine revs to the road speed and brake at the same time. That can be a big saving.

Back To The Brakes

Once you finish the drill, probably in practice, you'll want to start dialing in the use of the brakes again for the race. Start by using them very gently. When you come up to the turn, be in the position to just squeeze on the front brake. If you find yourself snapping at it, you're rushing yourself again. Remember, it isn't the guy who gets the brakes on last, it is the one who covers that part of the track in the least amount of time, which means at the highest rate of speed.

The front brake is a control.

A control is used to direct **motion**. You are directing the **speed** of the bike to match your **idea**. When you were doing it with no brakes, you took lots of time to make the change in speed. Now, you're doing the job in about one-third the time.

It works like this: Once you've braked to a speed close to what you want, you're using the last few feet of that braking to set the final **entry speed**. There you are, leaned over, making the final adjustment. With no brake you weren't leaned over and this period of adjustment might have been 50-150 feet. Here, you're doing it in 10-30 feet.

Chapter Recap

1. The brakes are used to "process" the bike's speed to match your **idea** of how fast to be going.

2. Your **sense of speed** allows you to adjust speed.

3. **Speed memory** is the key to consistency.

4. **Target speed** is the speed you intend to go at some part of the track. It is a projected **idea** of speed.

5. Not attaining your **target speed** for the entry to a turn creates a mistake. You can become trapped in a series of "corrections" in trying to make up for that mistake.

6. **Sampling** is the process that allows you to keep track of your **sense of speed** and **speed memory**. You use it to monitor speed, and decide if you've made your **target speed** or not.

7. Sampling is done by switching your **attention** back and forth from the **motion** that is taking place to the **thoughts** you have about this motion.

8. The No-Brakes Drill lets you spread out the period of **speed adjustment** so you can develop your **sense of speed**, **speed memory**, **target speed** and **sampling**. It frees up the attention you'd normally spend on braking. You're able to spend it on judging **distance** and **speed**.

9. Finding an **end-of-braking marker/area** will help. You have something to look ahead at, to determine whether or not the braking you are doing is correct. It also helps in passing other riders going into turns. With end-of-braking markers or areas, you can put your **attention** far ahead of yourself going into the turn. **You will not have to rely on brake markers.**

10. Your **sense of speed** needs to be developed in both accelerating and decelerating situations. Sense of speed is the most important ability a rider has. It allows you to change speed and gives you confidence.

Braking Checklist

1. Do you have an **end-of-braking marker** or area for each turn?
2. Are you having trouble reaching your **target speed**?
   a) Is the speed too low?
   b) Is the speed too high?
3. Do you feel "frozen on the controls" while using the brakes?
4. Do you feel rushed coming into this turn?
5. Are you relying on a **beginning-braking marker**?
6. Any problem with braking and downshifting together?
7. Where is your **attention** while braking for this turn? Is it:
   a) At the beginning of braking?
   b) In the middle of braking?
   c) At the end of braking?
8. Is your **attention** focused on:
   a) **Traction** while braking?
   b) **Braking force** (how much your body is pushed forward by the braking force)?
   c) Your **position** on the track?
   d) The **entrance** to the turn?
   e) Your **speed**?
   f) Your **plan** for the turn?
   g) Your **end-of-braking marker/area**?
   h) Working the **brake** lever?
   i) Working the **clutch**?
   j) Working the **throttle**?
   k) Working the **gearshift** lever?
   l) **Holding on** to the bike?
9. Are you able to **sample** — to switch your **attention** while braking?
   a) Are you able to keep track of your **location**?
   b) Are you able to keep track of your **speed**?
   c) Are you able to keep track of your **braking traction**?
   d) Are you able to keep track of your **control timing**?
   e) Are you able to keep track of your **lean angle**?
10. Can you spend enough **attention** on the **plan** and the motion?
    a) Do you have a clear **idea** of where you should be on the track while braking here?
    b) Do you have enough **reference points** to keep track of your **location** on the track?
11. When you think over this area of braking:
    a) Is it confusing?
    b) Can you remember it at all?
    c) Do you remember only a small portion of it?
    d) Does the time seem compressed?
    e) Does it feel like you have enough time?
    f) Does it feel like you have too much time?
    g) Can you imagine adjusting the speed?

12. Do you have a **target speed**?
    a) Do you have a good **idea** of how much faster it is than before?
    b) Do you have a good **idea** of how much slower it is?
    c) Do you feel like you can't reach it?
    d) Do you feel like you can reach it?
    e) Do you have enough **attention** to spend on it?
13. Is your **speed memory** working?
    a) Can you enter the turn at the same speed you've entered before, if you want to?
    b) Does your **entry speed** seem to vary a lot, lap to lap?
    c) Do you have enough **attention** to spend on it?
    d) Do you have enough time to get it right?
14. How is your **sense of speed**?
    a) Can you raise or lower your **entry speed**?
    b) Do you feel "stuck" on one entry speed?
    c) Are you giving yourself enough time to adjust it?
    d) Are the brakes on too hard for you to sense the speed?
    e) Is your **attention** somewhere else so you can't do it?
    f) Are you trying too hard?

CHAPTER IX

Corner Speed And Drive

The Use And Abuse Of MPH.

Adding speed through acceleration isn't always the hot tip.

In addition to timing and braking, there is another facet to controlling your speed while entering, going through and exiting a turn. This applies to most turns with the exception of wide-open and accelerating ones such as the high banks at Daytona.

Let's set the stage by saying that you just entered a medium-speed turn at, say, 75 mph. You make your major steering change going in, and just after that you notice that you could have been going 2-3 mph faster, or whatever a "little" faster is to you.

I've found out from asking and watching that most riders don't really notice if their speed is down until somewhere around mid-turn. **It takes some time for most of us to let everything settle down enough to get a good handle on corner speed**, and to make a judgment as to whether it was right, too fast or too slow. If it happens to be too slow, the usual immediate response is to try to make up for the low speed by getting on the gas harder than usual coming out of the turn. You've found a mistake, and you're trying to fix it while there's still time and track. Is this familiar?

Don't Look Back

Of course, the mistake has already occurred and there's no real way to make up for it. You have already shifted your **attention** from the **motion**, sensing your speed, to your **thought**, which contains your **idea** of how fast the turn could have been entered. At that point you arrive at that old feeling: You could have been going faster.

Whatever it feels like to you, there's usually some disgust attached to your feelings about that particular mistake, but that isn't the major problem. The thing that caps it off is that you have to make a new **decision**, an alteration of your **plan**, right at that place. That decision usually is to increase your drive. As slight as it might seem, it's still an alteration of a plan you had previously decided was the best way you could tackle that corner. How you originally intended to ride that turn must now be changed.

Most riders try to make up for low cornering speed with a strong drive off the turn.

If you get in too slow you grab too much throttle and slide.

This is the Plan that most riders have to make up for a slow entry. Does it really work?

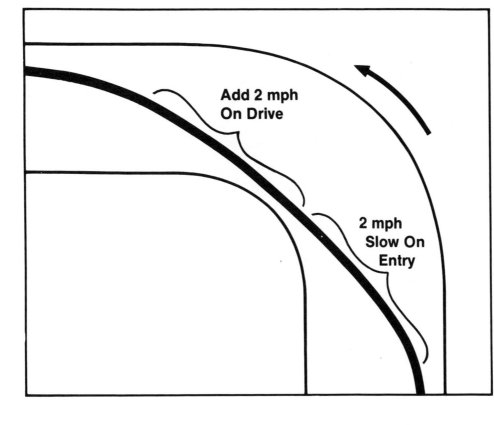

Add 2 mph On Drive

2 mph Slow On Entry

Low-Speed Problems

Throttle action is smooth with good entry speed.

Throttle action has spikes and changes when entry is slow.

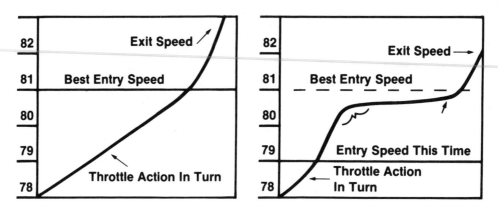

If you know what speed you want in a turn it really saves a lot of problems that will never even come up. If you get it right it is great. If you get it right!

What happens when you do this? This bike "will" accelerate at some rate coming out of the turn without losing traction, but now you're trying to make up for the speed you didn't keep coming in. You might be trying for an acceleration that the machine can't deliver as far as traction goes, and you might slide around a little, perhaps have to roll off the throttle or even get the **idea** that you can't come off that turn hard!

From another viewpoint, you are in the turn and your **attention** goes to **sampling** the **speed**. You temporarily forget about **traction** because the speed is too slow. You know from memory that the bike will go faster right here, and you can **sense** that as well. You make a quick calculation as to how fast you'd be going if you hadn't come in too slow, then add the drive acceleration to that. At that point, you're trying to deal with a big jump in acceleration, perhaps more than the tires can handle.

If you had done it right, and come in at the speed you wanted, you wouldn't have had to pass the **sliding threshold** while trying to make up for low corner speed.

The higher your cornering speed, the smaller the throttle action needed in the turn and at the point where you begin your drive.

Warning: New Decisions In Progress

You might also notice that most slide-outs are not on the entry to turns; they're in the middle of them. Slide-outs going in are usually caused by using too much brake, almost never by too much speed. Most mid-turn slide-outs, especially on production bikes, are caused by grounding out the bike's undercarriage, or ¡ust leaning it over farther than the tires can handle. But, why did the rider have to lean the bike over so far if it wasn't to compensate for the extra acceleration he was trying to get on the exit, after he came in too slow? That's not always true, of course, but think back on your own experience. Doesn't your **attention** switch over to the drive so you can make up for low corner speed?

Don't you find yourself in the middle of some turns just "waiting" for the place where you can begin your drive? Has this happened to you so often that you now believe it is the correct way to ride, and you just expect it to happen?

The new **decision** to increase the drive out, made after noticing the low entry speed mistake, is really the culprit here. It's a major change in the **plan**. You are trying to crowd two plans into the space of one turn — which doesn't work — or you are making up for no plan at all — which doesn't work either. Having no plan leaves the door open to all kinds of desperate riding techniques.

Going too slow in a turn creates more problems than going too fast. The one obvious exception to this is falling down from too much speed; but even so, more riders fall off trying to make up for low speed than fall trying to handle too much speed.

The Force

The forces generated by a motorcycle accelerating while leaned over are in the realm of physics, and you aren't going to beat physics at its own game. When you surpass the bike's ability to stick on the pavement by trying to apply an acceleration factor that's unrealistic, you're looking at a generally unwanted condition: Excess sliding.

Everyone who races agrees that sliding must be taken into account if you're going to be fast, but it must be **planned**, and it must happen out of choice, not out of desperation. If your original plan called for keeping your **attention** on a smooth drive, you were set up to do that. Changing to the hard drive is very different. There's no setup to make it work.

It's great to be able to get both ends sliding especially in turns with some banking. The bike just slows down and then it will take the throttle as you get to your right speed.

Do you recognize the situation of being in the middle of a turn and not feeling very good about turning the gas on, but at the same time feeling like you should be going faster? It's a problem you have made for yourself.

More Speed, Please

The concept of preventive medicine is to treat a person so that diseases don't get started. Preventive riding applies in the same way. You want to stop making new plans in the middle of turns to correct for mistakes in cornering speed. The solution is to come to turns at the "right" speed, which involves tricking yourself — or better — understanding the forces at work when you come into the turn.

103

If you're like most riders, you let the bike settle down as you enter a turn and "get the feeling" of the speed. The problem is that once you turn, the bike immediately starts scrubbing off speed because of the resistance and friction of the tires. The bike is trying to go straight, and the tires are taking the load of the steering change. So, while you "get the feeling" of the speed going in, you're sensing something in a state of change. The speed is dropping.

In order to hold the speed you have when entering a turn, you must apply throttle.

No Solution

Now you've got an **idea** about how to handle this problem, but you don't yet have a total solution. Start by getting the gas on as soon as you can after you finish braking or slowing down for the turn. It can be done, but you might find it difficult at first to be delicate enough with the throttle. The second part of the solution is to enter the turn a little faster, so the initial slowing down of the bike is already handled, and that will make your **timing** for rolling on the throttle a little less critical.

Entering a little too fast gives the rider some time to get the roll on started.

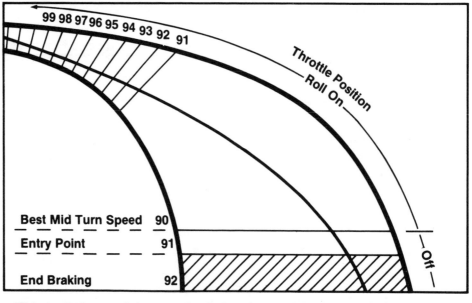

Going in a little hot is better because you can save them alot easier than you can on acceleration spin outs.

This technique might sound a little scary — and it is — but it does allow you to put your **attention** on the **thought** to work the controls rather than on the **motion** of the bike. It gives you some time to sort out the entry, and it doesn't leave you down on entry speed. It breaks down like this for most riders:

1. Let's say the bike will slow down 2 mph in the first 25 feet after turning, going into a 90-mph turn. After that, it slows at the rate of X mph per foot from there on until the point you have planned to begin accelerating.

2. Much or most of your **attention** is on your **entry speed** just before you make your steering change. That's correct; you are at the part of the turn where you'll make any necessary speed adjustments.

3. For a short time — really just an instant — you put your **attention** on the **steering change**. It costs you quite a bit of attention to make a

steering change. Many riders find that part of the turn actually blank in their memories. Is that true for you?

4. You spend some **attention** on getting the steering done at a particular spot on the track. That's already taken some attention away from sensing speed before you even turned. It's not so much the steering itself that chews up your concentration, it's setting the **lean angle**. That's the immediate result of the steering change. (The long-term result is your **direction**.) How much do you spend on this?

5. You've got some **attention** on the lean angle and some on the turn itself, then you shift back to the speed and try to get a handle on that. It's changing as you notice it, which makes the process more difficult.

It is harder to sense a change than to sense a constant. It's hard to judge speed when it's changing.

6. You get your **attention** swinging back and forth trying to plot the deceleration, and by the time you get it figured out, you're already at mid-turn! At that point, you've got the "mid-turn blues."

You had the speed set going in. You took your **attention** off the speed to get some other important things handled. You get your attention back on speed, and it's either changed or changing from where you left it. The time for fixing it has gone by, and you try to salvage the turn by turning up the wick on the way out.

You spend a lot of time judging speed when you are making any kind of change.

The Rider's Solution

After a rider practices this way of doing it for enough laps, it becomes his style of riding for that turn. He knows it isn't really right, but he can't change. This has happened to you, hasn't it?

Most riders do ride this way; you can see it and hear it. It might seem too simplistic to suggest that you enter the turn 1-2 mph faster so the speed will be "right" for the turn once you're into it, but it "will" work. Entering the turn "too fast" is exactly what you must do. Obviously, there is a limit. Not so obvious is the ease with which you can do it if you treat that tiny bit of time, when you set the speed, as something other than just "going into the turn." If you don't get it right, you'll pay for the mistake through the whole turn.

Coming into a turn, your primary concern should be how much speed you'll keep, not how much you'll get rid of.

Too Fast Or Too Hard

Part of the entrance problem is steering. Let's look at it more closely. There are two reasons for not being able to steer when you want to on the entrance of a braking turn: Going too fast or braking too hard. Most people confuse the two, but they're really separate problems.

If you come up to the point where you want to turn and you're braking so hard the fairing is on the front fender, you probably won't initiate the turn because the bike would fall. You're asking the front tire to carry two loads at once: Braking and cornering. At the extremes of braking and cornering it just won't work.

Get Off The Brakes

Which brings up an interesting point. If you come into a turn at a speed you think is too high, your chances of making the turn are much better if you let off on the brakes. Two things will happen:

1. You'll transfer some of the load to the rear wheel, giving you the chance of sliding the back end of the bike (and making it more controllable).

2. You increase the bike's ground clearance, allowing you to lean it over more and perhaps compensate for the extra speed.

Rider Adjustments

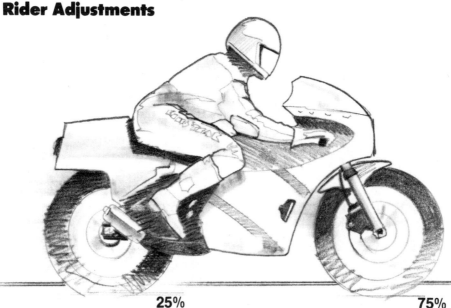

Trailing brakes into a turn loads the smaller front tire.

25%   75%

Weight Transfer

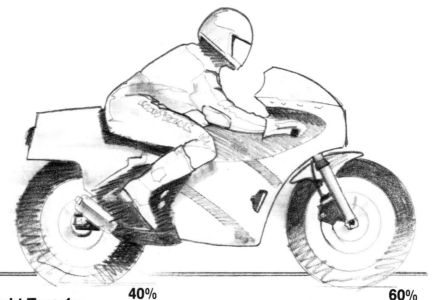

Getting the gas on soon transfers weight onto the larger rear tire.

40%   60%

Weight Transfer

The solution to this corner problem is to do what all the good riders do: Get on the gas as soon as possible. By doing so, you get responsive steering with weight transferred to the rear end when entering a turn.

With the gas on, you also pick up some ground clearance. Turning the gas on at the right part of the turn widens the contact patch of the rear tire, creating something of a "berm."

The hard part is making yourself do it. You have to enter the turn at a speed you think is a little too fast, then you have to turn the gas on! Logically, it all makes sense, but somehow, when you're in the turn, it seems so wrong. You're going too fast; then you go faster to handle it?

Note: If you've really misjudged your speed and you're going too fast for this technique to work, leave the gas off and just widen the turning radius. Just let the bike run out wide in the turn, scrub off some speed and make the best of it.

Entry Trick

You can trick yourself into entering the turn just a little bit faster without suffering a lot of fear. By simply turning up the bike's idle speed, you transfer weight onto the rear wheel as soon as you let off the brakes. Setting the idle up to 2500-4000 rpm will give you the same effect as turning on the gas, but you won't have to physically work the throttle right as you let off the brakes. You'll be surprised how easy it is to get used to it. You'll also pick up some ground clearance.

Turning up the idle buys you some time coming into a turn. You can be a little lazier in letting off the brakes and getting on the throttle. Part of the job is already done for you. You can spend more time — and **attention** — making the final adjustment to your **entry speed**.

You might want to always leave the idle turned up, or you might get the hang of what is going on and begin to set up for the turn so you'll have the gas on when you want it. Turning up the idle is just a trick.

Another Advantage

There's another lesson you should learn from the world's best riders: **Don't use the engine as a brake.** You don't hear the engine rev up to redline when you watch good riders come into a turn. They all do downshifting at the last possible moment so the engine doesn't rev too high. An engine at redline wears out rapidly.

The engine does give you a little cushion after you let off the brake going in.

Using the engine as a brake can cost you ATTENTION and $.

An engine at redline is also a distraction. Where does your **attention** go when the engine is spinning up there at 11,000 rpm? It's spent on the engine; if your attention is on the engine, it is not on your riding.

The best riders rely on the brakes to slow the bike. That's what the brakes are for. The engine, on the other hand, is there to accelerate the bike. If you use the engine as a brake, if you're working with that **idea**, then you also must believe that the higher the engine is revving, the better the engine brake is working! Far too many riders, even at the national level of competition, have got this same **wrong idea**, and it costs them a lot of money in blown and worn-out motors — not to mention blown laps.

Turning up the idle will help you to quit using the engine as a brake and will force you to rely on the brakes to do the job they are designed to do.

Mid-Turn Speed

Most of your mid-turn speed problems will be resolved by getting the entrance speed right to begin with. You should be able to make very small mid-turn speed adjustments with the throttle, up or down ½ mph, and begin to explore your maximum speed through a turn. You can't even hear that small a throttle change while standing next to the track. You can begin making fine adjustments like this once you have the **entry speed** right.

Suspended Speed

What is the right speed as far as suspension is concerned? If you were lucky or smart in setting up suspensions, you'd have a bike that, going in, slid evenly. The back wouldn't come around more than the front would "turn in." The bike would predictably slide both ends and would feel neutral while doing it. Once you were into the turn, with the gas on just a bit, that same bike would quit sliding the front, allowing you to bring the back end around with the throttle. That would be a nice bike to ride!

We're not talking about big slides here; big slides lose time. We're not talking about the bike sliding 1 foot off your line. We're talking about the tires giving up maybe 2 percent of their traction in an even, predictable fashion.

Fresh Rubber Please

If your tires are good for a given track on a particular day, you have the advantage of being able to ride with a controlled slide. In the turn, as you do a nice, even slide, you constantly expose fresh rubber to the track surface. You can only do it until the tires get too hot, at which point they begin to rapidly release the oils they are compounded with, and the tires become "greasy." Until that point is reached, the rider who can keep his tires clean has a much better traction situation.

The opposite extreme occurs when a rider is running too slow for his tires and actually picks up rubber from the track. The rider is not going fast enough to keep his own tires clean. That's OK, unless he gets into a turn way too hot and has to really use his tires. If that happens, the rubber on the surface will scrub away at an accelerated rate and he'll be doing some serious sliding.

There's another fascinating point to consider about tires. Most tire development is done by the riders who go the fastest. The tires are made for them, so they'll win races for their tire sponsor. If that rider uses this sliding technique, almost everyone else using the same kind of tire is riding on rubber that is overdeveloped for them. In this case, the slower rider would be much better off with a harder tire that would stay cleaner on the track.

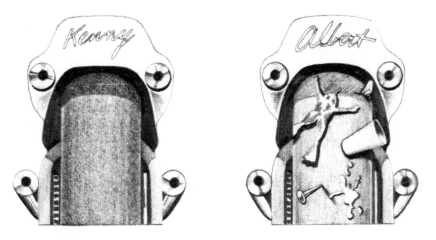

A tire that is too sticky but not used hard enough can collect things from the track.

Zone Of Speed

You can find a little "zone" on most bikes, somewhere between ½-1 mph, where the bike will do a nice, easy drift/slide. The tires aren't really sticking completely, but they aren't quite into a slide, either. In that zone lies **control**, and you control it with the throttle. You can't stay in that "zone" if you make big changes in the throttle, either on or off.

If you can get a bike into this zone, it will handle really well. It feels as if you have lots of control. If you've never gotten a bike into this zone, ask some good riders about it. They'll tell you that it seems as if the suspension has suddenly started to work right. And they'll also tell you that you'll never find that zone if you don't have your **entry speed** right to begin with.

The Drive

Now that you've got the entry speed right, and the mid-turn speed is in the **traction zone**, you should be all set for a good drive out of the turn. Two factors determine where you will start your drive: **Location** and **traction**. Your location on the track includes being able to see far enough ahead of you to be able to calculate how much throttle you can use, and how fast you'll be able to straighten the bike up. You have your **attention** on these two things; they are important.

You can begin the drive when you can begin to straighten up the bike.
At that point, you'll have more tire on the road (more traction) and a higher possible rate of acceleration. How much track you have to do that determines how fast it can be done. If you exited a turn in the middle of the track, you'd be able to accelerate the bike hard because you wouldn't require very much lean angle to keep from running of the track. If you came out of a turn all the way to the outside, you'd have to keep the bike leaned over to keep it on the track when you roll on the throttle. That's a function of the cornering forces at work.

The harder you accelerate, the farther out the bike swings.

Your Judgment

To start a drive, you rely on your ability to judge the distance you have to the outside of the track at your current turning radius, along with your ability to judge your rate of acceleration. Those two together determine your drive off the turn. One of the things that is part of "knowing a track" is the rider's ability to begin a drive before he can actually "see" where he is going to wind up. Narrowing it down even more, you can understand that your **sense of location** on the track is at the top of the list of what's important at this part of the turn. That brings you right back to **reference points** as an important factor in making a good drive.

You must know where you are before you can actually see where you're going.

Traction

Your **traction** is directly related to how straight the bike is. When you are really familiar with a bike and its tires, you'll know how much acceleration you can use at what lean angle. But, traction can be looked at in still another way for the drive off. Just as the mid-turn has a **traction zone**, so does the exit. You play traction against throttle at the exit of a turn:

1. You roll on the throttle and the bike's rear wheel begins to spin slightly.

2. You then pick the bike up a little to get the traction back.

You roll on the throttle and straighten up the bike all the way out of the turn to get the best drive. These two things happen at the same time; it isn't like holding some lean angle while waiting for the wheelspin, then straightening the bike up quickly to stop the spinning.

Gas Or Lean?

When you have to hold your lean angle, you cannot yet begin your drive.

If you're coming off a turn and you see you'll have to hold maximum lean angle awhile, you should also know that a hard drive off this turn won't work. You just aren't going to be able to compensate for the acceleration. If you are like most riders, you get yourself stuck in this

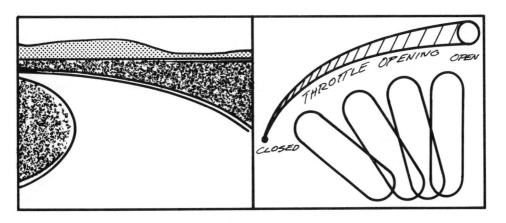

position frequently. You come to the exit and you can see your way out of the turn. You can't begin your drive, though, because the bike's still leaned over, and you can tell you'll have to hold that lean angle. This is familiar, isn't it?

Drive Timing

If there is a secret to getting a good drive, it's in that simple fact. **You can't begin a hard drive off a turn until you can begin to straighten up the bike.** Don't even upset yourself, as most riders do, by wasting your **attention** on wanting to turn on the gas when you can't. When you can straighten up the bike, you can roll on the gas. That's all there is to it.

Your job is to find the place to do it. You have to keep the **mid-turn** and the **exit** separate in your mind because they are very different. It looks like most riders begin to anticipate the drive out well before they get to the place where it can be done. That is one of the reasons you see and hear the throttle applied on in the middle of the turn, then hear it backed off a bit before the drive begins. I'm not saying that you shouldn't experiment with the drive to see where it can be started, but **there is a place to start the drive and beginning too early creates a problem**.

You shouldn't even think about accelerating when leaned over. If you accelerate at all it's just a fraction because it's going to spin.

When you anticipate the drive off and begin too soon, it commits you to leaning the bike over even farther, which will foul up your drive. That's a **timing** problem. It becomes an **attention** problem as well, because you can't really spend a lot of concentration on "wanting" to turn on the throttle when it isn't time yet. Spending your attention on something that isn't happening creates confusion. It's like "hoping" the tires won't slide or waiting for them to slide; you put a lot of **attention on nothing**. That means you can't concentrate on anything else, such as your speed, lean angle, location and the rest. You don't have to hope you'll get a good drive; you just have to **time** it right.

Chapter Recap

1. Slow corner **entry speed** can cause a series of problems for a rider throughout the entire turn.

2. Riders often find themselves going slower in the turns than they want to.

3. Riders generally try to make up for low corner speeds by increasing the drive off the turn.

4. With the correct entry speed and cornering speed, the rider can use smaller throttle adjustments throughout the turn, reducing the possibility of sliding out.

5. Low entry speeds cause the rider to shift his **attention** from what he should be doing to how he will make up for the low speed.

6. Designing a new **plan** to handle too low a speed costs time and distance on the track — and plenty of **attention**.

7. Compensating for low entry and mid-turn speed is more likely to make you fall than handling too much speed.

8. When a rider practices a series of mistakes enough times, it becomes his riding plan through that turn.

9. The basic solution to the problem is to enter the turn a little too fast. That compensates for the speed scrubbed off by the cornering forces while you turn.

10. Getting the throttle turned back on as soon as possible puts the rider back in control of the machine. Better **weight transfer, cornering clearance, throttle control** and **traction** are the positive results.

11. Staying off the brakes going into a turn you enter too fast gives you a better chance of not falling or making more mistakes.

12. A useful trick is to turn the idle up to 3000-4000 rpm, allowing the bike to maintain speed when entering turns.

13. Many riders have the wrong **idea** that the engine is a brake. Using the engine as a brake creates many more problems than it solves.

14. How your bike handles and where it slides, are limiting factors in how fast you can go. A little drifting and sliding is good for a variety of reasons.

15. Riding style has a lot to do with tire choice and tire performance.

16. There is a **speed zone** in a turn — the perfect balance of tire traction and speed — in which the bike will work its best.

17. Your drive off the turn is determined by where you are on the track and by how much lean angle you're using.

18. The drive is a balance between straightening the bike up and applying the throttle.

19. The more upright the machine, the more throttle can be used.

20. There is a **traction zone** in turns that the rider creates with lean angle and throttle action which offers good control.

21. An effective drive cannot be started at maximum lean angle.

22. Beginning a drive too early is a common mistake and creates its own problems.

Speed Checklist

1. On which part of the turn are you having problems with **speed**:
    a) Just before you begin to steer?
    b) Right after you begin to steer?
    c) Right after you finish steering?
    d) In the middle of the turn?

e) Just before the drive begins?

  f) Just as the drive begins?

  g) In mid-drive?

2. What is the problem?

  a) Too much speed?

  b) Too little speed?

3. How are you handling the problem?

  a) Rolling off the gas?

  b) Rolling on the gas?

  c) Leaving the gas alone?

4. Is what you are doing making the situation change?

  a) Is it getting better?

  b) Is it getting worse?

  c) Is it staying the same?

  d) Can you tell if it is changing or not?

5. Where is your **attention** just before you notice this problem with speed?

  a) Is it on **traction**?

  b) Is it on **lean angle** or **ground clearance**?

  c) Is it on using the **controls**?

  d) Is it on your **location** on the track?

  e) Is it on your **body position**?

  f) It is on the **engine**?

  g) Is it on the **cornering forces**?

  h) Is it on the **deceleration forces**?

  i) Is it on something else (asphalt cracks, bumps, etc.)?

6. Where should your **attention** be so that you can get the speed right?

  a) Are you leaving yourself enough time to sense speed?

  b) Is there enough time to set the speed?

  c) Do you forget about speed altogether?

7. What changes are you going to make so that speed isn't a problem here anymore?

  a) Change where you were spending your **attention**?

  b) Change what you do with the **controls**?

  c) Change both your attention focus and control use?

8. What is going to happen if you make these changes?

  a) Will you have to lean the bike over more?

  b) Will you lean it over less?

  c) Will you be able to hold your old line?

  d) Is the bike going to slide some?

  e) How much throttle will you be able to use?

   l) Is that more or less than you've been using?

  f) Will you have to change your braking?

  g) Are you going to need some other reference points?

  h) Will you have to change your body position?

9. Can you see your **plan** working out?

  a) Does your new plan make the problem easier to think about?

  b) Does your new plan just create more confusion?

10. How much time do you think you will save by changing this?

CHAPTER X

Riding Plans

A Style For Every Rider. Try One On.

By watching a rider and what he does, you can figure out where he has his attention and how much attention is being spent on what. You can figure out his plan.

Study the plans and decide which ones you use.

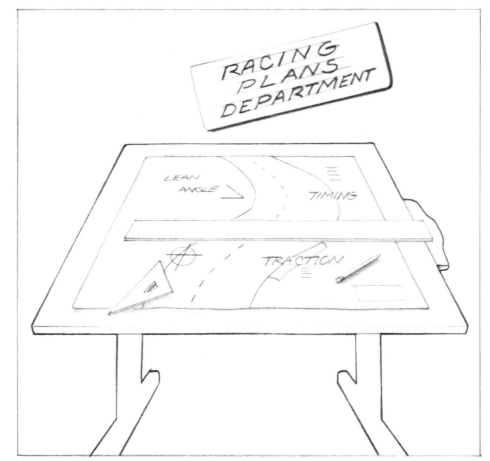

There are lessons to be learned from examining the different riding styles. As you progress, you will build your own **plan** based on where you can spend your **attention**, on sensing the **motion** in front of you and the bike going around the track, and on monitoring your **thoughts** and **ideas** on how to do it. That's your plan.

Two distinctly different PLANS for the same turn.

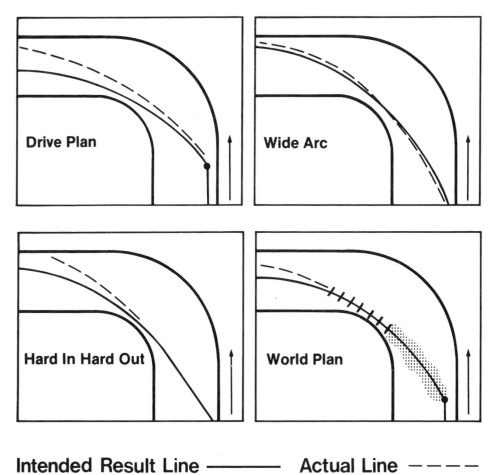

What you want and what you get are determined by your plan.

Drive Plan

Wide Arc

Hard In Hard Out

World Plan

Intended Result Line ——— Actual Line – – – –

The Drive Plan

Let's take up the riding **plan** that made Kenny Roberts famous in the U.S. and was the foundation for three World Titles. Not only was his original style easy to observe, he's also told us the details of his **plan**. He said the emphasis was on the drive out of the turns, and he shredded enough tires riding that way to prove it. He also told us that he used a "studied" entrance into the turn — giving up some of the **entry speed** he could have used in favor of getting the bike pointed in the right direction — to get out of the turn with maximum throttle. In dirt track terms it is one of the applications of a technique called "squaring off" the turn.

"Squaring off" a turn in dirt track. This IDEA works in road racing as well.

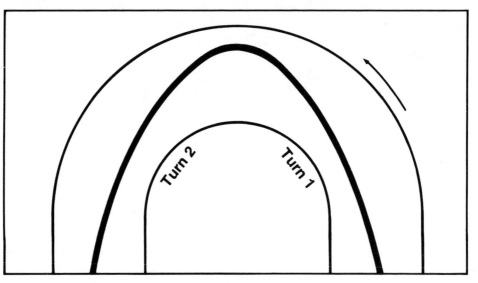

The application of this technique isn't the same for every turn. Why would you want to make a mid-turn steering change in a fast turn? You wouldn't. But, keeping with the **idea** of getting the drive, you can still design your entry for that purpose.

As with most **plans**, this one is fairly simple to describe. Basically, you set your line up so that there is a definite steering change somewhere in the turn. If the turn is long or has a double apex, you can go in a little hot, allow the turn to scrub off some speed, then get more of the turning done at the lower speed, and "point" the bike straight on the turn's exit.

The goal is to allow the bike to be as upright as possible when you exit, so you can use maximum throttle. You get the turning done so you can concentrate on the drive out.

Note: Before I get too far with this description, I want to point out that without the horsepower to make this technique work, you're generally wasting your time. The Drive Plan won't work well with a 600cc production bike because the machine simply lacks the motor to drive hard coming out of most turns.

What's The Plan?

In using this **plan**, most of your **attention** will be spent getting the bike in position for the steering change. That will be the object of everything you do while coming into the turn. Adopting the Drive Plan for yourself would require thinking out the entrance and the mid-turn so you could get positioned right. You need a very accurate mid-turn turning point, and you want to avoid big speed changes right at that point. The mid-turn steering change makes this an energetic riding style because the rider must resteer the machine mid turn. This style allows the rider to take more time setting the speed of the machine going into the turn. In a double apex or decreasing radius, it's the mid-turn turning point that's the critical part.

If the entry speed is too great, the steering change can't be made, or it will take longer than necessary — and then you lose the drive. If the entry is made too slow, you give up what you might have gained by using this plan in the first place.

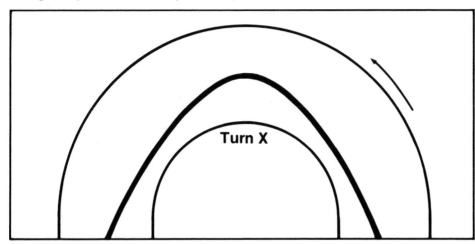

Turn X

The "Squaring off" might look the same on asphalt. The road racer can go in deeper.

Studied Entrance

A "studied entrance" doesn't mean a "sloppy entrance"; you still must be precise. It means that you're not going so fast that you can't make the corrections you'll need to get a blistering drive off the turn. If you enter a turn as fast as the bike can go, you'll have to stay committed to that line, missing your opportunity to "set up" the drive.

The good part about the Drive Plan is that the turn is broken down into two distinct parts: Entrance and exit. A great benefit of this style is that **traction** and **lean angle** are not used to the maximum during the "studied" part of the turn, leaving your **attention** free to do the "studying."

Juggling Your Attention

Breaking this plan down into **thought** and **motion** shows its real brilliance. By keeping the speed down at the entrance, a rider can put more of his **attention** on the **plan**.

The more speed you add, the more attention you will spend on sensing the motion of the bike.

By not adding more speed you have more free attention to put the bike exactly where you want it and get it set up very precisely. You get the turning done and everything ready, leaving you with most of your attention free to sense the tire slippage while you're exiting the turn. The plan was set at mid-turn, and the rider uses all his attention to get a good drive. **Going in, most of your attention is on the plan; going out, most of your attention is on the motion.**

What the rider does is juggle his attention from the thoughts to the motion, back and forth. In the Drive Plan, the rider chooses to spend attention on **accuracy** and **setup**, then juggle it back to sensitive throttle application, wheel slippage and raw speed. You can have a terrific plan for any turn, then make it fail by adding speed at the wrong place. It shifts you away from the plan and onto the speed.

Try and get most of the attention juggling done in practice, get your plan set and then you can keep track of it easier when the race comes.

The Drive Plan By Pieces

Here are the main pieces and parts that you will need to adopt the Drive Plan to your own riding. It is especially effective in double-apex, decreasing-radius, and banked turns of "medium" speed. You need:

1. A good idea of where the turn goes, especially the radius changes Increasing (IR), decreasing (DR), constant radius (CR). By understanding the exact shape of the turn, you can figure out where you want to go and how hard the drive out can be.

Example: In a DR turn, you have to wait to turn much later than in an IR turn.

2. An exact place on the track, a **reference point** (RP), where you will make your mid-turn steering change — where you will "square if off." (You'll still need an accurate turning point going into the turn.)

3. Some spare **cornering ground clearance** at the place where you turn. (If you are leaned over all the way, you won't be able to turn the bike any more sharply than it already is, unless you slide the back.) This is for a mid-turn steering change.

4. The speed set so that you can turn where you want to. Going too fast at the mid-turn steering place will draw out the time it takes to get the bike turned. However, using this technique, you usually don't have to make a fast steering change at the entrance, and you can actually bring up your entry speed by not being leaned into the turn as much as possible.

5. The last major factor is **control**. The Drive Plan technique will not work, or might make you feel uncomfortable, if the bike is bobbing up and down from harsh use of the controls. You can't go into the turn and pull on the front brake to get the bike turned. You must have the speed adjusted evenly with the throttle, making very small changes in throttle position, especially for a mid-turn steering change.

Plans Again

The faster you go the more you have to pick up your reactions to what's happening.

Keep in mind what we're trying to do by examining these different riding techniques. We're establishing where you will have to put your **attention** in order to make each technique work. Also, you should be able to look at your own riding to determine where you are now spending your attention. What kind of **plan** you develop will be determined by where you can, or will, put your attention.

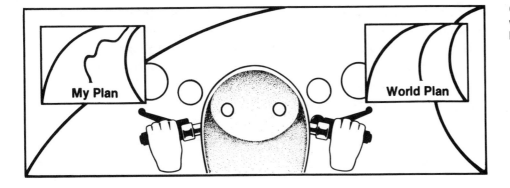

Comparing these plans to what you are doing can help.

Wide Arc Plan

The Wide Arc Plan is based on carrying maximum lean angle and speed through a turn. Using this technique, you enter and exit the turn as wide as possible. This plan doesn't call for mid-turn steering changes, as a rule. This plan produces, on paper, the straightest line that can be drawn through a given turn.

Wide Arc Bills

What it will cost to make this plan work is constant monitoring of **lean angle**, **speed** and **line** at almost every instant throughout the turn. This type of plan appears to be the smoothest, but in fact it has the rider juggling his **attention** back and forth the most.

Do you follow how it works? You come into a turn and get the bike over to **maximum lean**, then you want to keep track of that very carefully. **maximum speed** always burns up a lot of **attention**, but it's part of the plan, too, so it must be taken into account. These two factors bring up another: **Maximum traction**. You'll be looking for maximum traction everywhere and that costs plenty of attention as well. Since no major and very few minor steering changes are called for, the **line** is critical from the beginning and must be monitored very closely. The rider constantly spends attention on these four factors: Maximum **lean angle**, maximum **speed**, maximum **traction** and **ideal line**. He's unable to let go of any of them for any length of time. If any of the four demand additional attention, the rider is forced to let one of the others slip somewhat.

The rider who uses the wide arc plan must look even further ahead on the track than with any other riding plan.

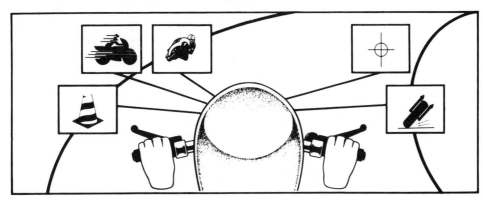

The WIDE ARC rider must keep his ATTENTION on more all the time.

Currently, there is only one national-caliber rider who's had any ongoing success with the Wide Arc Plan. It's Mike Baldwin, with four Formula I titles to his credit in the U.S.A. However, after one half a season on the GP circuit in Europe, his riding is changing away from this style.

Wide Arc Thought And Motion

The rider is attempting to spread out the turn as far as possible to gain time and distance. He tries to slow down the scene in front of him so he can fit in all of the constant changes in **attention**. He attempts to limit one factor, **steering changes**, to the minimum amount of attention, so the other areas like **lean angle** and **speed** will have most of his attention. The major drawback to this technique is that it demands the highest thought output from the rider, never allowing him to put full attention on any one factor for very long.

There's nothing "wrong" with this plan for certain applications; just as the Drive Plan has both strong and weak points, so does this one. The one great fault of this plan is that it doesn't make use of the capabilities of modern race bikes to their fullest; it would never win a World Championship in Formula I. On the other hand, while the Drive Plan won't work well for underpowered bikes, the Wide Arc Plan will. Because he can't make a tire-shredding drive on a small bike, the rider must determine to keep his cornering speed high to win.

Wide Arc Plan Parts

1. A **line** that has the least amount of variation (steering changes) in it at the entry, middle and exit of the turn.

2. Excellent **reference points**, so you can best monitor your **location**. The better the RPs, the more **attention** you can spend on looking after the **speed** and **lean angle** — the two other major ingredients.

3. Along with good RPs, you'll have to become comfortable with looking well ahead of yourself, farther down the road than most riders are used to. You have to look farther ahead with this plan because of your commitment to **lean angle** and **speed**.

4. Good **throttle control**. You can't make big changes in throttle position because this plan calls for **maximum lean angle** and **maximum speed** throughout most of the turn.

5. The ability to use the whole track on turn exits. You'll have to become acquainted with that last outside 2-3 feet of pavement at the exit because you'll need to use it. Work up to using every inch of the track, which is uncomfortable for most riders at first.

6. Don't confuse this plan with the Drive Plan. You aren't going to get any blistering drives off the turn; you're relying on your ability to keep the speed high through the "whole" turn.

7. Your **attention** is on balancing **speed** and **traction**. This plan doesn't call for any loss of traction (sliding) which would require steering changes to correct for the changes in direction of the bike as a result of the slide.

Hard-In, Hard-Out Plan

Most riders at club level (though there are some at the national level, too) have only one real plan: To go into the turn hard and come out of it hard. You might call this the "Hard-Up Plan" because, for lack of anything better, the rider simply breaks the turn down into its two most obvious parts, going in and coming out. He tries to go as fast as he can at two points. These two **ideas** are in conflict with each other.

Very little thought has gone into such a plan and the rider suffers from it; his **attention** isn't directed at any one thing at any particular time. This is really an **idea** that never made it to the planning stage of turning **motion** into **thought**.

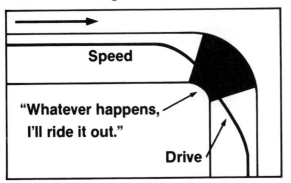

The hard in-hard out PLAN fails to take the mid-turn speed into account and doesn't have any set up for a hard drive out.

The Hard-in, Hard-out plan is really no plan at all.

The Hard-In, Hard-Out Plan has one major characteristic: Plenty of rough mid-turn corrections. You can see it for yourself at any racetrack, but I suspect that everyone knows what I'm talking about here, perhaps even from personal experience. You come into a turn with nothing but speed on your mind, and right in the middle of the turn there seems to be a lot to handle. "Of course," there's a lot to handle. You had to use up all your **attention** on the speed (motion) of the bike and none went to any plan of action. You were lost in mid-turn and you had to correct. **All those corrections take up time, they take up distance and they lose speed.**

You Forgot To Look

The biggest reason that riders keep on riding this way is that they're so busy handling all the problems they created that there's no free **attention** to put on observing whether what they're doing is working! If your goal is just to stay busy on a bike, that's OK, but if you want to win, forget the Hard-In, Hard-Out Plan.

Inspired Riding

There's little in life that is true all the time for everyone; that's the case in racing, too. There are riders who have a terrific amount of drive to win and to go as fast as the competition and they can make this plan work. It can also be noticed that these riders take a long time to get going fast at the races. They don't start to ride fast for quite a few laps. They almost never go fast in practice unless there's a lot of it. Feel familiar?

The hard in hard out plan is hard to ride around because these guys are the ones who change just as you are going to pass them.

The few who have had some success with this style just squeeze themselves into the go-fast mode, and find a way to connect the fast entry with the exit while tacking on some good mid-turn speed. These guys have to work very hard because 80 percent of their **attention** is on a **plan** that doesn't really exist. Not having a good, solid plan is like not having a place to live. It consumes your **thoughts** and you're always wondering where to go next. There are no rest points with this plan. It is even more attention-hungry than the Wide Arc Plan.

Hard-In, Hard-Out Plan Parts

You probably don't need any help figuring out the parts to this plan. If you've ridden without a good plan in the past, this is probably what you used. It's not a plan, it's an **idea**; one comprised of three parts:
1. Go in hard..
2. Come out hard.
3. Be willing to slide around and upset the bike.

The World Plan

The most precise riding style developed to date is the **World Plan**. It's a **combination of styles**, and it takes advantage of all the advances that have been made in motorcycle suspension and tire technology. It takes advantage of the good points of both the Drive Plan and the Wide Arc Plan, and adds some on top of that. It isn't a plan for the weak at heart, because, from a rider's point of view, **it's fairly complicated**.

Naturally, each rider has his own **ideas** on how the World Plan will work for him and what he has to do to make it work. From talking to Freddie Spencer and Kenny Roberts, it's hard to tell they are involved in the same sport; they each think about racing and what they do in entirely different ways.

Even though the results may be similar, riders have different ways of riding and thinking out their PLANS.

122

Common Denominator

No matter who you talk to among the few who can do it, they all agree that the plan involves five basic ideas:

1. Come in hard.
2. Go deep into the turn before steering.
3. Maintain high cornering speed.
4. Get a good drive out.
5. Use precise machine control.

It sounds like the plan that everyone should have, but only a handful do.

In short, this plan involves going fast everywhere in the turn. I call it the World Plan, because it is the only overall **plan** of riding at this time that would ever get you a World Championship title. It is the minimum ante for the game as it is now being played. You need five aces to open.

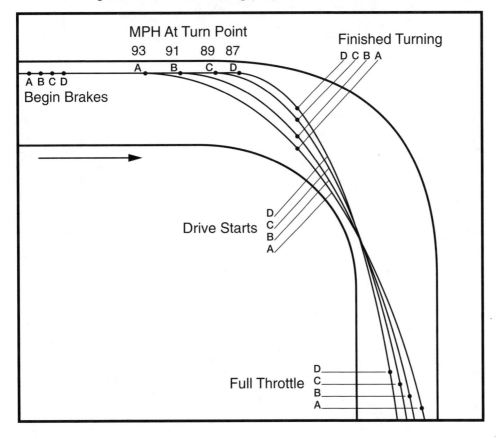

The basic idea behind early and deep turn entry and how it affects the drive.

Short And Sticky

Chassis technology comes into the picture. The relatively short-wheelbase bikes are the result of the development of tremendously rigid frames; the bikes don't have to be long to be stable any more. Additionally, with the rigid frames, the machines can be set up "softer" and still retain suspension characteristics. These two examples of modern motorcycle technology allow for even faster turning and more mid-turn maneuverability because a shorter bike requires less space and less effort to turn.

Older technology was limiting for the rider.

With modern technology you can ride any plan you like.

Tires figure into the equation strongly, as well. These days, tires are custom-made for new bikes, and help to compensate for the short wheelbase by remaining pliable enough in turns to keep the bikes from dancing around on rippled surfaces. Shorter-wheelbase bikes are inherently less stable than their longer counterparts, and tire technology has gone into making the newer equipment work. Tire technology has always seemed to be one step behind chassis technology, especially in Formula I bikes, but also now with 750 superbikes.

Rider Technology

In one application, the World Plan breaks down each turn into smaller parts. By making a series of adjustments, the rider can maintain higher speeds on the average throughout the turn. For example, if your **plan** dictates that you lean the bike over all the way right from the start — which most riders do — your **entry speed** must remain steady. If you leaned it over only 95 percent of the maximum, you could make speed changes.

The World Plan rider leaves himself some options on making steering correction. With the Drive Plan, you attempt to make a drastic steering change in the entrance or at mid-turn. With the Wide Arc Plan, you commit yourself from the beginning to maximum lean angle and speed. The World Plan takes the theory of the Drive Plan and spreads it out. Sometimes the bike is leaned and steered again, mid-turn.

Machine control is difficult when maximum speed and steering (lean angle) are being used.

If you can leave yourself the option of 2-3 percent lean angle to plan with when going through a turn, you can always correct your steering. With no lean angle available, you only have sliding as your last resort for steering changes, or you can roll off the gas. Allowing the bike to get "loose," but not sliding, makes mid-turn steering easier.

Control

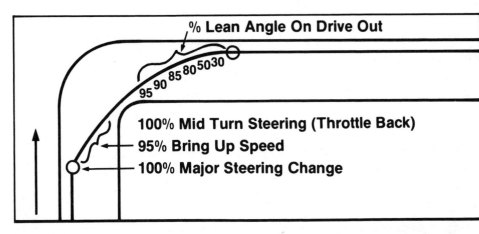

Making several changes in lean angle and throttle settings in a turn make it a precise style. The control timing must be correct for it to work.

According to Freddie Spencer, the World Plan leaves room for both steering and throttle corrections. While making these corrections is complicated, the additional control it allows can be productive. You can see that the Drive Plan would not work if the rider was already at maximum lean. The main reason riders can't make either of these plans work for them is their **idea** that the bike must be at maximum lean angle to be going fast. Even at max lean, the mid-turn steering can be done if the throttle is rolled back some right as you turn it more.

If you can make a throttle or steering correction you have done all you can do.

World Gas

The World Plan overcomes many problems by having the rider on the gas just after braking and turning is done, transferring weight to the rear of the bike where it won't cause problems for the time being. The front end has far less tendency to "push" (slide) when it isn't loaded. Transferring weight to the rear tire has a further advantage of **traction** because of the tire's larger contact patch. There is yet another bonus: increased **lean angle ground clearance**.

Throttle Limits

If you have the option of rolling the throttle on and off a little, you have that much more control of the bike.

When you can't make throttle or steering correction, the bike is out of control.

Unplanned sliding is a good example. When the bike is sliding, you can't do much of anything with the steering or the gas. Almost anything you do will make the situation worse, unless it is done gently.

If the back end is sliding and you roll off the gas, it serves to further lighten the rear end, possibly increasing the severity of the slide. Conversely, if the tires are working, and you aren't leaned over all the way, you can roll on the gas and transfer more weight to the rear, getting it to "hook up."

Once the gas is off, you can't make any further corrections in that direction. You can't roll it off any more.

Control = the ability to make steering and throttle changes.

Dirt Track Road Racers

Dirt trackers make good road racers because they understand mid-turn corrections.

Road racers believe mid-turn corrections are a nuisance. They usually force themselves into do-or-die mid-turn crises, and they acquire a bad taste for these corrections. Dirt track riders accept them as a fact of life. They use those corrections to make up for changing track conditions. They seem more adaptable as road racers because of this ability to correct. A dirt track rider's **plan** leaves room for mid-turn corrections; they are his ace in the hole.

Slide Steering

Some guys get to a slide in the wrong part of a turn and you can see they are out of control. Stay away from them.

Slide steering is the technique of changing the line of the bike without steering or leaning over more. It's simple to describe: You slide the back out a little and the bike is then pointed a little more toward the inside of the turn. You're then able to begin your drive earlier in the turn. You're also going to be able to begin to pick the bike up earlier to get the - **traction** advantage of the bike being more upright.

If you've ever watched Kenny Roberts race, you know that controlled sliding of the rear is an important part of his **plan**. He says that if he didn't slide the bike going onto the banking at Daytona, he would hit the wall! For him, sliding isn't something nice to do every so often; it is absolutely essential to the game as he plays it.

Out Of Control vs. Control

At its extremes, the bike is out of control.

No matter what overall **plan** you're using, the idea of **being in control** is still correct. On the other hand, if you assume that sliding the bike is part of control, that you can slide where and when you want to without a violent reaction from the bike, you can walk a fine line of **control/out of control**. The hard and cold fact is this: You will have to learn to walk that fine line if you want to be among the best.

Past the fine line and into the heights of control we have our world class riders using the rear brake or the clutch to get the back end to come around. Yet another neat innovation to get the bike turned and ready for the drive out.

Technology Helps

Modern motorcycle technology goes a long way to help the rider maintain that fine balance. Improvements in suspension have assisted in the development of the World Plan; this particular technique also has been improved by the broader powerbands of modern machines.

A broader powerband doesn't make a bike faster, it makes it more controllable.

Control is the name of the technology game.

The rider uses this increase in control to go around the turns faster.
Note: It's obvious that the top riders are willing to be "out of control" at times. They can and do put out 110 percent, if necessary. The big difference is that they can "choose" their time and place to do it because they are using the extremes as tools, not as last resorts.

Plans

You use them all but mostly I use the world plan.

A **plan** is only as good as it handles the turns; your riding is only as good as it handles the plan. You must be able to control the bike to make your plan work.

In this case, the **World Plan** has 4 major parts or **ideas** that the rider must fit together with his **plan**.

1. Come into the turn hard.
2. Go in deep.
3. Have high corner speed.
4. Get a good drive out.

The **plan** will consist of steps the rider will take to control the speed and direction of his bike, to make those 4 things happen.

The World Plan calls for the rider to have his **attention** on **speed** and **control**. It is similar to the Drive Plan in many respects. The major difference lies in the entry and mid-turn speeds. They are the key to it, so that is where your attention should be spent. We are looking at medium speed turns since there are more of them.

1. The turn is entered at slightly less than maximum lean angle. Your entry speed can be higher because the bike is not at maximum lean. Using a banked 80-100-mph turn as an example, you can get a quick "snap" steering action going into the turn. As the banking increases, you'll also have to lean the bike over more to take full advantage of it. (On the exit, you'll have to straighten the bike up as the bank flattens out.)

Note: If you are using sliding as a turning technique, it is always "safer" and easier to slide the bike on banking than on the flat, because the banking offers some resistance to slides, making them more controllable. On a flat turn it is more difficult to keep control.

2. The throttle is on smoothly, almost immediately after the brakes are released. Weight transfers to the rear tire and you have **throttle control**. If you enter the turn with the throttle off, you rely on the front tire to carry most of the load, and it is smaller, offering less traction than the rear.

3. You can employ one or more mid-turn steering changes depending on the turn. The World Plan differs from the Drive Plan in this respect. Instead of making one great steering change, you make more, smaller changes, using maximum lean angle at several places rather than all at once. In mid-turn, you won't have to give up as much speed to make two — or more — small steering changes as you would to make one big one. Slicing the turn into smaller pieces allows you to move your **attention** back and forth (**sampling**) rather than having it stuck on one thing. Rolling off the gas a little with the steering changes makes them easier to do.

(To make any mid-turn steering change work, you will have to make throttle changes that complement them. Leaning the bike over to max lean means that a slight roll back on the throttle will have to be done. As the bike is set up again the throttle can be rolled back on some. Timing the steering and throttle changes to work out is what makes it complicated.)

4. Mid-turn steering changes need to be made well in advance of the

point where your drive out begins. You are trying to get the speed as high as possible just as your drive begins, so the throttle action and acceleration do not have to be so sudden.

5. Mid-turn acceleration from the last steering change to the point you begin your drive out of the turn. If you had this action timed perfectly you'd be at maximum lean angle right before you begin your drive, as you roll on the gas, you'd start to straighten the bike up. On the exit you will have some lean angle and throttle as control options. That gives you both of your control factors — **steering** and **speed changes** — to handle the exit. (Most riders get the drive going while the bike is still leaned over all the way, which limits how hard they can accelerate. They lose one of their control factors.)

Average The Plan

The World Plan averages out the extremes, not depending on any one part of the turn to make the plan work. It takes into account each section and how it will fit into the next. One of the things that makes this plan complicated to perform is the fact that you must make steering and throttle changes at the same time. That alone isn't a problem, but keeping track of the **speed** and **traction** at the same time makes it hard. However, the results in mph are worth it.

Rider Education Note: Again, our purpose in looking over these riding styles is to find out where the rider is spending his **attention** on **thought** and **motion**. When you understand that, you can adopt one that fits your own riding and bike. Better still, try all of the styles to get a good understanding of their strong points and weak points for you.

Chapter Recap

This chapter puts a lot of the other stuff together and recaps it all.

1. You can observe what a rider does and figure out how he thought out that section of the track.
2. Riding can be broken down in to general **plans**. This chapter describes the basic plans that are in use today.
3. The way you see the track and think about it will eventually evolve into one or a combination of these plans. Starting out with a basic idea of how it has been done in the past may be of help to you.
4. The Drive Plan is aimed at setting up the turn so that maximum acceleration can be used coming out.
5. The main emphasis is to get the steering done in mid turn to allow the rider max tire on the ground by setting the bike more upright.
6. Some speed has to be sacrificed going into the turn so that the goal of the Plan can be accomplished.
7. The Wide Arc Plan has the fewest amount of changes for the rider to make.
8. The rider using this style does have to pay for keeping those things constant. He is dealing with Max speed and max lean angle for most of the turn. His ability to make changes is reduced and the degree of accuracy he must use in Location on the track is increased.

9. This Plan is probably the easiest one to get started with and works very well with low horsepower bikes.

10. The Hard in, Hard Out Plan is the one most riders use but it really isn't a Plan at all. It is two Ideas put together with some bravery added to stick it together.

11. Riders have had success with this style but they have had trouble fitting the pieces together and generally are inconsistent. They are really working with a Plan that doesn't exist.

12. The World Plan is really a combination of styles and uses parts of the other three but puts them together with precision.

13. The World Plan is partially a result of modern day technology and has been developed to take advantage of both tire and suspension capabilities available today.

14. The techniques involved in this style break the turn into smaller parts and specific control operations for each section.

15. Control of the machine is maintained by not using the extremes except when necessary. Mainly max speed in conjunction with max lean angle are avoided

16. The World Plan is difficult because of the changes the rider must consider. In some cases sliding the bike is used to position the bike on the track and is included in the style, not as something nice to do but as a necessary part of the Plan.

Plan Questions

1. Which of these Plans best describes your riding?
   a. The Drive Plan?
   b. The Wide Arc Plan?
   c. The Hard in, Hard out Plan?
   d. The World Plan?

2. Which Plan, if any, are you using in the turns you have the most trouble with? (Choose one turn to think about)
   a. If no Plan is in use, which of the above would best handle those situations?
   b. If you are using one, what are you doing to keep it from working?
   c. List the exact changes you can make to improve the situation and make the Plan work. (Take one turn and sketch out what you are now doing and what you think will work)

3. Which Plan, if any, are you using in the turns you do the best with? (Choose one turn to think about)
   a. Have you got all of the pieces worked out or did you just fall into the style of riding it?
   b. Would one of the other styles work even better?
   c. Can you actually make another style work?
   d. Would you have trouble making that style work?

4. Is there some skill you would have to have, that you don't now, to fit yourself into another style of riding?

For example:

    a. Are you accurate enough with your location to be able to use the Wide Arc Plan? Can you comfortably use the whole track?

    b. Can you "square off" turns by making mid-turn steering changes?

    c. Do you need to get the feel of the bike sliding if you were going to use it as a tool?

    d. Is your sense of lean angle good enough to know whether you are using 90% or 100%?

    e. Can you "snap" the bike into a turn when you want to?

5. Is it easier for you to "set it and forget it," like in the Wide Arc Plan?

6. Can you see yourself making the steering and speed changes necessary to use the Drive Plan or the World Plan, if you wanted?

7. Is there some Idea you have that might keep you from changing your Plan?

    a. Your just out to have some fun riding and don't really want to get into it. (That's OK, by the way)

    b. You never did any dirt tracking so you couldn't learn how to slide around if you needed to.

    c. You are too old to change your style.

    d. You don't get enough track time.

    e. Your eyes aren't that good.

    f. It wouldn't feel right.

    g. You can't ride right hand turns as well as lefts.

    h. You can't ride left hand turns as well as rights.

    i. You are too big. (You can't be too small)

    j. Your bike isn't that good.

    k. ??

Homework

Take each turn or section of a track and figure out which Plan you are using.

a. Decide, for each of those turns, whether you are using the right one or not.

b. Use Chapter XI to fix any problems you have with it.

How To Supervise Yourself

Cheap Thrills. Go Faster For Only Pennies A Day.

I like this chapter, it lets you figure out your problems. If there is something wrong you can get it easier by concentrating on it.

Only a few riders in any racing era are able to break through the barriers and come to grips with their riding. Not only do they ride well, but usually there's some innovation in riding technique that is credited to their account. But innovation, in and of itself, is no guarantee of going fast, nor is it necessary to go fast. Some of the very top riders have merely refined the techniques of others, adapting them to their own riding — with very favorable results. Whether you're the rider who first develops elbow-dragging or not, there are three ways to go about shaping up your riding. All of them work, and all of them are used by the best.

1. Lots of **laps**.
2. Lots of **thought**.
3. Lots of **laps** and lots of **thought**.

There are a few people you could discuss your riding with. Talking and thinking it out.

In number 1, you don't have to be reminded of the expense of cutting lots of laps, I'm sure. It costs money to go to a racetrack, unless you have a sponsor; it also costs time. **The value of lots of laps is that they give you the opportunity — lots of times — to make hundreds of decisions about basic riding**.

The second way to improve your riding — **lots of thought** — costs not much more than the time involved to do it. In fact, if you've got limited track time, the second choice is really your only hope for serious improvement. While it's difficult to figure out how something "feels" by merely thinking about it, deciding what order things happen in and how much **attention** to spend on them is relatively easy.

In the third method above, you've got the best of all possible worlds. Plenty of laps and plenty of time to think about how things went, and to change things until you get them right. Unfortunately, this choice is out of the reach of most riders; about your only hope for this method is to get a factory ride, own a racetrack, or just to be rich.

Slippery Thoughts

This still boils down to the rider **translating** his riding (**motion**) into **thoughts** and back into motion again, no matter how much time or money he has; and thoughts can be slippery little devils. You could arrive at a "wrong" conclusion after a race, then think it out for hours until the next time you got to the track. You'd still be working with a wrong **idea**; it would just be well thought out!

Thoughts don't cost much, but even so, they often aren't worth the space they take up. What is needed is a form that can be followed, so that you aren't just shuffling thoughts around in hopes of coming up with good results the next time you ride. Like keeping a record of the checks you write, you need a way to keep track of your **thoughts** and of the **attention** you spent.

The Attention Line

Where you spend your attention is what you are doing.

In a turn, you do things to the controls of the bike. You make changes to the bike based on what you think should be done, and while you're riding, you **sample** what the bike is doing so you can tell how everything is — or isn't — working. If your **attention** is on **speed**, you adjust the speed or leave it as it is. If your attention is on **lean angle**, you change that or leave it alone. If it is on your **line**, you either change that or you don't.

To unravel any part of a turn, whether it's a problem or not, all you have to do is go back over it, pinpointing where you spend your attention. You had your attention on something, and you'd better be able to look over your "movie" of what happened, and come up with a good account of where you spent it.

Once you remember where you spent your attention, you can begin to sort out that area.

You spend ATTENTION on everything you do. Remembering where is the key.

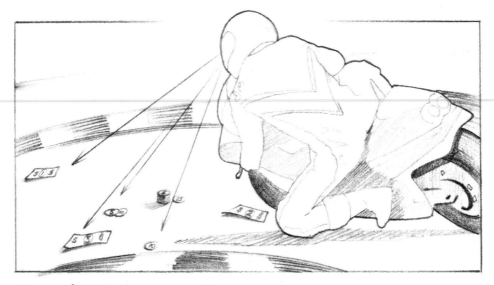

Attention Taxes

It's a lot like doing your taxes. You try to remember where you spent your money and you hope it was tax deductible. If you just forget about where your money went, and you're audited by the IRS, the auditor isn't going to accept your version of things. He'll want receipts. It's the same with racing: You'd better have receipts for where you spent your **attention**.

Attention Receipts

Fortunately, there are only five important places where a rider spends his attention, the **5 senses of riding**.
1. Speed.
2. Traction. (Braking, accelerating and cornering)
3. Lean Angle.
4. Timing.
5. Location.

At tax time, you divide your receipts into categories such as food, clothing, medical costs, shelter and so on. If you're missing receipts, it can drive you crazy looking for them. Losing **attention receipts**, or just not being able to remember what exactly you did, does the same thing.

Each aspect of riding can be found in one or more of the above **5 senses**. When you look back along your **attention line** to one or more of them, you'll see exactly what you were doing.

Example: You come into the pits and go over a turn in your mind. You discover that you had your **attention** on an old oil spot from the last race. The pavement is stained and that catches your attention. You look over that area and decide that the spot hasn't got anything to do with the way you're riding that turn. "Bang," you put that attention back in your pocket and spend it on more important things.

Unless your mind is wandering off to something else while you ride, these are the five things that occupy your attention. If there are other things on your mind, such as a fight with your girlfriend or problems at your job, maybe you shouldn't be racing that weekend.

A turn is just asphalt until you sort out where you are spending and where you will spend your ATTENTION.

Where To Search

The most effective way to improve is to find and handle the areas that are troublesome.

When you come off the track after a race or a practice, you'll have a feeling about what turns are giving you trouble. Something about this or that turn just wasn't right. That's where you look.

You just go along and pick up these problem turns and sort out what confuses you. You know those turns are confusing, because they got your **attention**. By contrast: **When you look at the turns that are going well, you will find very little attention "stuck" on them.**

That's how you get better. Figure out what you did that works in one spot or another.

Attention Experiment

Right now, look over a turn that's giving you trouble. If you're like most riders, you'll have more than a little trouble in doing that (Chapter XIII contains "Troubleshooting Questionnaires" for use in sorting out problem areas like this.)

It's hard to look over problem turns.

Now, look over a turn that isn't giving you any trouble. Chances are that you can track your **attention** and where you were spending it much more easily. Can you?

At tax time, it's easy to track regular expenses like your monthly rent check. You pay it on the first, and it's $500. And the time you blew your engine and had to pay $700 to get it fixed is something out of the ordinary, so you'd remember it, too. But, you might not remember all the little costs that went into fixing the engine: You spent $100 on valves, $125 on bearings, another $75 at a different shop for valve grinding, $250 at the crank shop, and so on. Riding can be similar. When you can't track what you did, it's hard to sort things out. There's some confusion. **A lot was spent, but on what?**

Tracking Your Expenses

This chapter lets you figure out where you are having the problem.

There are several reasons a rider can't remember clearly just exactly what he was doing in a turn:

1. **Attention on too many things at once.** Here, the rider hasn't

decided what's important and what isn't. Consequently, he gives equal importance to two or more of the **5 riding senses**. The rider finds himself looking at perhaps all 5 senses and not paying attention to any one of them to get good information. The result of this is confusion and, usually, a feeling that you're "frozen at the controls."

Example: The rider has just passed someone going into a turn. He has spent so much on the pass that he tries to get all of the 5 senses working at once to get a handle on how things are going. He lost track of them and feels the effect of it. It's like being lost and trying to go in all directions at once.

2. **Attention on the wrong thing.** The rider is simply spending his attention on something that has very little to do with what he's doing. For reasons known only to himself, he thinks they're important.

Example: The rider is looking at the pavement stain from the last race when a quick steering change is more important. He needs to have his **attention** on **location** and **timing**. That stain was important last race when it was slippery, not now.

3. **Out of sequence.** Attention that's out of sequence is similar to attention that's on the wrong thing. The major difference is that the rider just puts what he's doing out of order with what he is **sensing**. (Most often, the rider gets too far ahead of himself. Less frequently, he still has his attention on the last turn.)

Example: In another example of a quick steering change in a braking-turn situation, the rider knows what's coming up and gets ahead of himself by anticipating the steering changes. He forgets to set the speed, and tries to do it after the steering change is made. Of course, it is then too late.

4. **Attention stuck on the controls.** Working the controls of your bike produces the **speed** you sense, the **traction**, the **lean angle**, and your **location** on the track. Where and how much you use the controls will determine whether things work out as you planned. The **where** and **how much** constitutes your **control timing**. Working the control itself takes up some of your **attention**. Leaving your attention on the control is a mistake. It promotes the **idea** that you get information from the control, but you don't. **You get it from what the bike is doing in response to your control actions.**

Example: Most riders spend too much **attention** on the throttle. There you are in a turn "looking" at your hand on the twistgrip. What's more important, the speed or the twistgrip? The same goes for the handlebars or the clutch. If you get your attention stuck on them, you are starving more important items.

5. **Too little attention on the controls.** This is the opposite of No. 4 and the result is **poor timing**. You aren't getting things done when you need to; they usually are done too late. You may need to spend a nickel's or a dime's worth of attention on getting to the control you are going to use, just before you need to use it.

Examples: Reaching up to put one finger on the clutch lever toward the end of the straight, before you downshift, costs little **attention**. But, doing so sets you up for easy use of that control. You're in touch with one of the next things you have to do. In the same way, having your hand in position to roll on the gas when you're finished with the brakes saves having to reposition your hand at that critical part of the turn. It also serves as a good reminder to start turning it on when you want it because half the job is already done. Likewise, putting your foot up to the gearchange lever saves a tiny bit of foot movement later, and lets you feel in advance what you'll be doing next. Moving your body into the position you'll want in the turn "before" you get there helps, too. This doesn't work with all riding styles.

Attention Trouble

Your attention is on something.

You're looking at something all the time when you're on a racetrack. Maybe it's a **reference point** or a spot on the track that makes you feel uncomfortable. Maybe a bump that gives you trouble is the focus of your **attention**. Perhaps you're trying to decide what will happen next: Is traction OK over the next patch of ripples? Can the bike be leaned over any more? Will your speed run you off the track?

Note: Attention and sight are not always the same thing. You can be looking at one thing while thinking of another. On a bike, you mainly use your sight to determine **location** on the track. Traction, timing, speed and lean angle, the other **4 senses** of racing, aren't determined by sight alone. No sight is used to sense **traction**, for instance. On the other hand, sight plays an important part in **speed**, if you have an end-of-braking marker. There, you're using your depth perception to keep track of the available distance you have to set the speed of the bike.

Problem area = attention on the wrong thing.

Taking a look at any trouble spot is as easy as asking. "Where am I spending my **attention**?" Every time you find an uncomfortable track situation, it can be unravelled by following your **attention line**.

You want to be able to have the whole track feel good.

Missing a Reference Point because your ATTENTION is on traction is an example of a mistake.

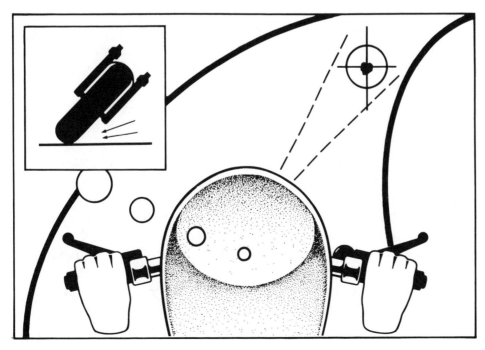

Control Attention

What you are doing with the controls ought to have something to do with what you want done at that time.

All too often, I hear riders complain about not having enough cornering speed; then they find out they're not even on the gas at that point, or they might even still be on the brakes!

Example: You're in the middle of a turn, and you have your **attention** on **lean angle**. You have the **idea** that your drive should begin somewhere around a certain point. The lean angle takes up so much attention that you can't get to the drive. You don't have enough attention left over to move your hand on the throttle until you take your attention off the lean angle!

Problem: As you ride over a bumpy section of the track, the bike slides and you don't like it. It happens to be toward the end of a turn where you think your drive should begin. When the bike slides, you're upset enough that you aren't able to get back on the gas, even though the traction is good after the ripples.

Solution: Locate the bumps "exactly," so that you can roll back the throttle just enough so the bike isn't spinning its rear wheel as you ride over the bumps. Time the throttle roll-on so that the bike is in the power just as you clear the rippled section.

Result: You use the parts of the track which offer good traction, and you handle the poor traction without cutting down on your speed. You don't upset yourself. You keep the bike under control.

Ideas to change: Probably your most bitter enemy in overcoming a situation like this is your own **idea** that you should be on the gas when you make your drive out of the turn. After all, that's usually the correct condition to be in at that point. In this case, it isn't, and you're just going to have to weigh the good points of this change against that basic **idea**, to see if increased control and eliminating the distraction of sliding adds up to a better ride for you.

Decisions that work: You aren't going to be able to simply decide to go out and ride faster. In fact, doing that will usually slow you down. You'll be able to go faster if you take the time to decide where you will make control changes and how much **attention** it's worth.

Attention Budget

If you budget your attention like the federal government budgets its money, you're going to be in trouble. The government decides what it wants, then goes into debt to get it. You can do the same thing. You want a new car, so you get a bank loan. You don't take a vacation that year, and you stay home most of the time, but you've still got the car. In riding, as in the above example, you put lots of attention on lean angle and miss the drive. The government, on the other hand, doesn't stop doing anything it did before; it just prints up more money. You can't print up more money, just as **you can't spend more attention than you have**. The most successful businesses have a real budget, as do the most successful riders.

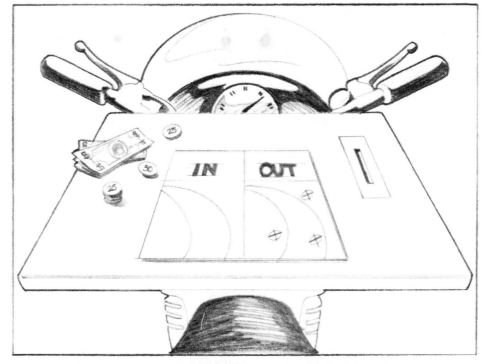

Making the decision to "go faster" is the same decision the government makes each year. But how are you going to pay for it? Anyone with any sense knows that a budget is based on earnings, and it's used to determine what can be spent. In riding, you decide what is important about a certain part of a turn; then you figure out where your **attention** is and whether it can be better spent somewhere else.

You must determine where you will spend your attention and what you will get back for it.

Like doing your budget, you take care of the rent, phone, utilities, food, clothing — the important things — then you look at what's left over for entertainment. In a turn, you decide where the **5 senses** are best spent, in what order you should spend them and how much on each. If you find some **attention** left over, maybe you can "buy" another ½ mph, or maybe you just save it. On the straights, you save most of it.

Attention Broker

There are two ways to spend **attention**:
1. Maintaining the **motion** of the bike.
2. Investments in **future motion**.

In real life, most of your money is probably spent on those things which maintain a certain standard of living. Food maintains the body; shelter, water, gas, electric power and the rest do the same job.

Maintenance on a motorcycle, from a rider's point of view, is that which he has to do to keep the bike going, either down the road or around the track. Investments with **attention** are those things that can be done beforehand to improve something later on in the turn.

Let's take a look at a turn to see how a rider might **plan** where his **attention** will be spent. We'll catalog which things are investments and which are maintenance.

139

Attention Planning

As an example, say you're on a 150-mph straight and are approaching a turn that can be taken at about 75 mph. You have to use the brakes. You're in sixth gear, and you'll have to come down to third for a good drive out. The turn is a left-hander with 10 degrees of banking to it. There's a short straight after the turn, so you can get the maximum drive without having to worry about getting the bike set up for the next turn.

Approaching this turn, on the straight, you can relax and take a few deep breaths. You can stay tucked in, but that shouldn't cost much in the way of attention.

As you draw near the area where you'll begin your braking, you spend a little of your **attention** on your **location**. You can **pre-position** the bike, right to left, so you won't have to handle that later on. That's a **wise investment** and easy enough to arrange. Next: Getting a good visual fix on your **end-of-braking marker/area** will let you know when it's time to begin the braking.

Just before you start to brake, you can put your body in position for the turn itself — **another good investment**. If you don't get your body over (if your riding style includes hanging off), you'll have to spend something on body position just at the end of braking, or wherever you switch body position. There isn't anything "wrong" with waiting to hang off, except that doing it beforehand **cuts your cost of attention** later on in the entry.

You spend a little attention on making sure you're firmly anchored to the bike, with the least possible amount of pressure on the handlebars. Perhaps you hook your leg around the tank, or squeeze onto the bike in some other way. On a GP bike, you can just move up to the tank which will support you. There's a little problem with this, though, considering which part of your body is against the tank when you're straight up. If you move over to hang off, your thigh is against the tank — much better. Now you're in position and ready for the brakes.

Investing your ATTENTION in the future can allow you to keep things separate and stay ahead of yourself.

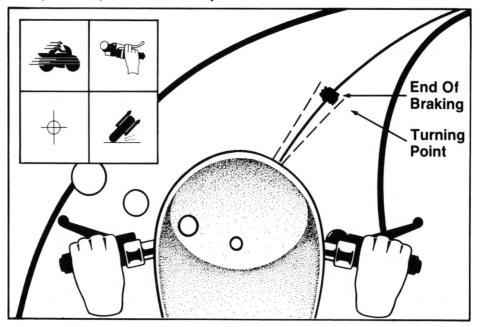

End Of Braking

Turning Point

140

Keeping track of your end-of-braking marker/area gives you a running record of the amount of space you have to set your speed for the turn. You are spending your **attention** to **sample** it. You use your **depth perception** to gauge that distance. **This is an investment** because the outcome of how well you keep track of it will determine your **entry speed**.

Keeping track of the amount of **braking force** gives you some indicator of how hard you can brake. That's important; you don't want to lock up the wheel. Keeping track of braking force isn't, however, an investment; it's maintenance. You're just paying your rent.

Note: Ultra-late braking is like a loan. You borrow from the amount of time and distance you have to set the speed of the bike comfortably, and pay it back in increased **attention** on that very hard braking. Slightly early braking is like spreading a loan out over four years instead of two. The smaller payments allow you to buy more things in the meantime. It costs you a little more time to do the braking, but taking the time to get the speed for the turn set properly might buy you more in **cornering speed**, which you can carry into the next turn. If you work it right, you can get paid back with interest.

OK, now you've applied the brakes. You brake the hardest at the beginning. From experience or just understanding the physics involved, you know that you can't leave the brakes on as hard at 75 mph as you can at 150; the wheel will lock up. As the bike slows down, some of the weight that has been transferred to the front wheel returns to the rear. The front becomes somewhat lighter and can lock up more easily. All of this means that you'll have to adjust the lever pressure as the bike slows down. This costs some **attention**. (Theoretically, you'd have to constantly adjust the brake lever pressure in order to keep up maximum braking force throughout the braking action.) If you've got your **attention** on the **braking force** right to the last instant of braking, you'll lose track of the **speed**; the speed is more important toward the end of braking.

Good planning would include being able to spend most of our **attention** on **sampling the speed** in those last few feet of braking. Bringing the braking force down to say 90 percent of maximum will allow you to spare the attention to do that. Leaving the braking force at maximum won't.

As all of this is going on, you still have the job of **downshifting**, which must be fitted into the picture as well. You want to fit it in so it demands the least amount of **attention**. **Downshifting is like paying your electric bill:** You want the lights to work when you come home, and you want power when you roll on the throttle.

Downshifting toward the end of braking, when you're backing off the brake lever, will allow you to use some of the spare **attention** you have at that point. Downshifting while you're braking at maximum decreases your ability to brake well.

The longer you take to **downshift**, the longer you must spend **attention** on it. Downshifting is an unpaid debt until it's done. If your plan includes three shifts, and you do them quickly, you can get back to the more important jobs at hand. You have a choice on how to pay — all at once or on time. Paying all at once means you'll have no payments later on.

At this point, the hard braking and downshifting are done; you're in position on the track (right to left); your body's in position on the bike, and you're keeping track of both your end-of-braking and turning markers. Now you come to the hard part: Setting the speed and turning the bike. Both of these are very important. Which one is the most important? Where and in what order will you spend your **attention** to make the **entry** work? You have some choices.

Where you begin to roll on the throttle, and how hard you can turn it on, come from the investments you have already made in **planning** your **line**. Investing in a lot of **lean angle** means you'll have to wait to begin your drive. Investing in getting the bike turned as soon as possible, so you can begin to straighten it out, gets the drive started sooner.

Plan #1

You can finish braking before you turn. In this case, you spend your **attention** getting the speed right, finish that job completely, then switch over to getting the turning done just where you want it. It's a plan.

Plan #2

You can begin to turn while still setting the speed with the brakes, finish setting speed while leaning the bike over, and continue to lean over until you've attained the turning radius you want. That works, too.

The simplest way to enter a braking turn. It's really a PLAN for spending ATTENTION.

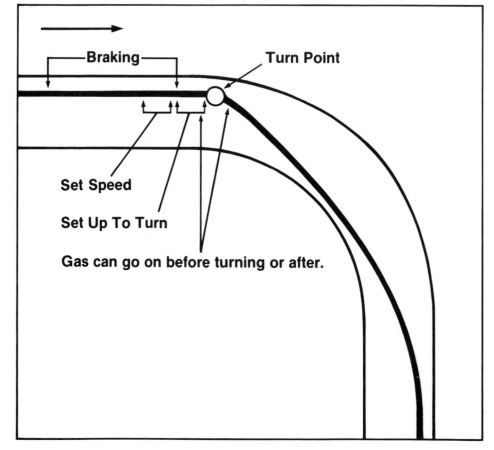

Braking

Turn Point

Set Speed

Set Up To Turn

Gas can go on before turning or after.

From the standpoint of spending **attention**, Plan 1 is easier. Plan 2 requires that you **sample** both **speed** and **location** at the same time. Obviously, good riders can do this with skill. Even if you've been using Plan 2, perhaps you should switch to Plan 1, if you're having problems with the **entry** to braking turns. Plan 2 is actually an advanced riding technique, but it's not the only way to ride a turn.

Sub-Plan

In addition to the basic parts of both of these **plans** is the question of throttle action. When are you going to get back on the gas? For Plan 1, you can turn the gas back on (crack it open) before you even begin to turn. You can also wait to turn it back on until after you turn. Either way will work, but either will cost some **attention**, too. You could have trouble spending attention on this if you do it before the turn. For most riders, getting the gas on "after" they turn is easier. Which way do you do it? You can try both.

There's not much choice on where you apply the throttle with Plan 2 because you're still braking after you begin to turn. Also, you might find it hard to turn on the throttle while you're still turning. If so, you do like most riders: You wait until the steering is done before using the throttle.

At this point, you're in the turn with the gas back on. The bike is leaned over and you can see whether your **entry** was to your liking or not. You might be able to make small changes in your **line** at that point, but no big ones. There's no point in spending much **attention** on your line now, except to notice where you are on the track so you can change it next time if you need to.

Traction is generally the information you want most when you're done with all of the other business of the turn entry. Spending attention on traction is just maintenance. You're already in the turn and you try to make the best out of what you have. Keeping the bike at or near the **traction limit** is the best thing you can do for your line. You won't get ahead by paying for traction information; it's like buying car insurance: It doesn't make the car run any better or make it worth more. It just makes you feel safer about driving it.

The obvious exception to this statement is when the rider loses traction on purpose to get the bike turned more to the inside. This gets more "steering" done at one time, so the drive can begin earlier. That's an **investment in future traction and location**.

Traction Or Speed?

The actual **speed** of the bike is something that can be overlooked while the rider has his **attention** on **traction**. You could say that speed doesn't really make much difference if you're getting the traction right, but that's not quite true. Spending something on **sensing** the **speed** allows you to get to the traction you want more easily when you're in that same section next lap. Sensing the speed gives you the "lead in" to the traction limits, and allows you to keep your attention free until you approach the speed that's close to that traction limit.

143

Without a good sense of speed, you must keep your attention on the traction most of the time.

If you've found a spot that has poor traction because of ripples or different pavement or whatever, a good fix on the speed "before" you enter that section allows you to be able to predict what will happen. If you know that you're going a little faster than before, you can expect more of a slide. Keeping track of the speed is a good investment.

Drive Attention

As you approach the exit of the turn, your **location** on the track again becomes important, because what you do with the throttle will change your **line**. **How much throttle you can use depends on how much you can straighten up the bike.** If you are still pointed to go off the track, then it wouldn't be a good idea to do either one of those things. This is the place in a turn when you play **traction** and **location** and **speed** against one another to come up with the best drive. **Your location determines your speed**, so location is the best investment you can make at the beginning of the drive. Once you're satisfied with the location (line), return your **attention** to **traction** and how much **acceleration** (speed) you can use. As you make the drive, it will pay to do a little maintenance on your location now and then so you'll feel safe. You **sample** it briefly after you make some increase in speed.

The more unfamiliar increases in speed you make, the more you will need to sample your location on the track.

And now, you're through the turn. Nothing to it. When you're on a budget, you have to decide which bills to pay and when to pay them. Once you have a schedule (**plan**) set up, you always know how to cut up your paychecks.

Sampling Budget

Just to refresh your memory, **sampling** is when you use **attention** to **sense** something, then measure what's happening against your **idea** of how it should be going. When you cut back your attention budget on any of the riding factors, there's a snag you can run into.

The less you sample something, the more it seems to change.

Example: You are in a long, fast, decreasing-radius turn. As you come to the part that decreases, you let the bike run to the outside of the track to set up a good drive out. Your speed and position on the track make your **sense** of **location** important. It is so important that you forget about **sampling** the speed for a while. When you return to the speed, it has changed enough so that you aren't familiar with it anymore and it's usually too slow. You weren't paying attention to it, and it changed a lot.

Solution: Whenever you find yourself losing track of one of the **5 senses** you must **plan** to **sample** it more often. **The more often you sample something, the easier it is to keep track of it.**

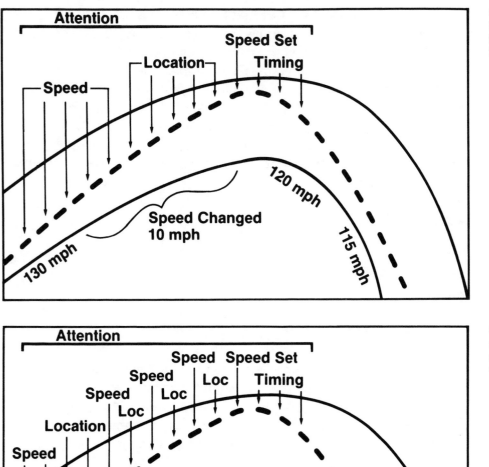

Attention

Speed

Location

Speed Set
Timing

120 mph

115 mph

**Speed Changed
10 mph**

130 mph

Only SAMPLING location, forces the rider to try and set the speed and timing all at once.

Attention

Speed

Location

Speed

Loc

Speed

Loc

Speed

Loc

Speed Set

Timing

120 mph

115 mph

**Speed Changed
2 mph At A Time**

130 mph

SAMPLING his SPEED more often, this rider is ready for the steering point with his speed set right.

Pay On Time

There's something else happening here that you must take into account. You can't stare at your turning point right up to the time you actually begin the turn. You'll need to switch your **attention** from that point, before you get to it, so you can see where you're going in the turn. Making this switch properly requires **timing**.

Even if you say you don't really have a turning point, you still set yourself up to turn at some place. And the better a rider is, the more consistent he can be. The point is, **attention and sight shift into the turn before the actual turning is done**. So, what can go wrong with that? Timing wise, two things:

1. You look into the turn too soon.
2. You look into the turn too late.

145

In #1, looking too soon, you might turn before you reach your intended steering point. Turning 5-10 feet too soon will radically change how the turn must be ridden. Looking too soon changed your **line**.

The second example is one of spending attention on the turning point, right up to the point when you actually turn, and it will probably make you get into the turn too slow. In this case, you haven't looked ahead and that makes it hard to judge how fast you can go. You slow the bike down just a little more to make the speed feel "safe." You looked ahead into the turn too late. This same idea could apply to the drive or throttle changes in esses.

Force

There is, in addition to the 5 senses of riding, a **force** that riders (you) spend **attention** on and it may be a source of confusion for nearly everyone.

Physics To The Rescue

As you turn, there is a force generated from the bike wanting to continue in a straight line. You are steering it to the right or the left and as the bike turns it "pushes" you down in the saddle and compresses the suspension. **That force is increased or decreased in any turn depending on how quickly you make the steering change.** Gradual turning yields less initial force than does a quicker steering change.

You can run almost the same line with a quick turn as you can with a slower one but the initial FORCE is much greater.

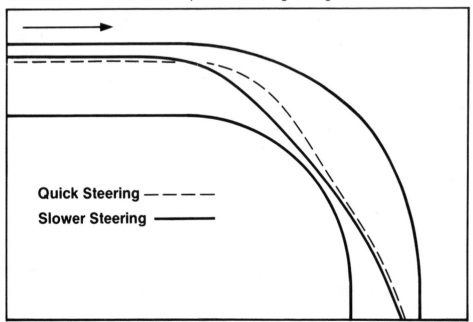

Quick Steering — — — —
Slower Steering ————

The **force** you notice entering a turn will be the same for any particular speed and turning point. In other words, if you approach a turn at 103 mph on the same line and turn at the same point, and same lean angle, lap after lap, the amount of turning cornering force will remain the same. But, if you change the way you steer into the turn each lap, that initial **force** will be different. Could this confuse you and tempt you to think you entered a turn slower of faster than before? It could.

Force Distraction

Riders who can turn quickly and use it as a tool have been able to sort out the **force** from the actual speed of the bike. It is a very similar situation to **braking force** and **speed**. Your **attention** goes onto the wrong thing and it goes on to it for the wrong reason.

Having your attention on the force does not give you the information you are looking for at that time. You want to know if your entry speed was OK or not, yet there you are **sampling** the cornering **forces** generated by the kind of steering change you made.

That quick **sampling** of speed after you turn will have a lot to do with how much or how quickly you get the throttle turned on.

While the FORCE of turning is happening you should keep your ATTENTION on SPEED.

Armed Forces

You are attacking this turn. You must be armed and ready to handle the throttle play you will need to keep up your mid-turn corner speed. The **force** generated from turning will go away right after you turn but the speed you are carrying will last until the **drive** out. That short moment when the **force** is high can get your **attention**, you might even become fascinated with it because it is something of a "rush."

Battle Plan

Riders who don't "like" high forces generated by quick steering are likely to turn in more gradually. The way you enter turns right now probably has something to do with your experiences with the **force**.

Be ready for the **initial cornering forces** but be prepared to ignore them in favor of having your **attention** on the **actual speed of the bike**. That should be part of your **plan**.

The Costs Of Spending

Road racing motorcycles cost the rider. Not only does it generally drain his wallet, it's not unusual to find yourself mentally drained at the end of a race. The concentration involved in directing one's **attention** in the focused manner racing requires does something to people. It can get to you.

Poor physical conditioning can contribute to the problem. When you become physically tired, the first thing to go is your sense of **timing**. When a rider is tired, his lines get "soft"; he doesn't turn as crisply anymore, throttle action becomes more abrupt, and the riding no longer flows from one action to the next.

Why the riding suffers is not really a mystery. If you follow back on your **attention line**, you'll see that your riding becomes poor because you have attention concentrated on your body.

If your attention is on your body, it is not on your riding.

Ideally, you wouldn't have to place any attention on your body at all. You'd just give it one command to turn the bike, and it would make each action exactly the way you want. It would be just like your bike: When you turn on the gas, you expect it to go, and just as with your bike, if your engine misfires, your **attention** is switched to the machine, and the rest of your riding suffers.

State Your Case

Best time to think about it is going to the race or at the races but there is a lot you can get done between times too.

If you were going to state the whole subject of racing as a problem to solve, it would go something like this:

Overall view: How do I win races?

Rider's view: How do I ride through a particular turn in the least amount of time?

Aside from having a competitive bike, you require certain things to answer that question:

1. Know each turn layout perfectly.
2. Always know where you are on the track.
3. Know which control to use for each riding situation.
4. Know how much to use each control.
5. Know exactly when to use each control.
6. Stay on the racetrack.
7. Have enough control for the next section, (if they are connected).
8. Complete each lap.

9. Be able to change plans, lines or procedure, at will.

10. Improving lap time (continued learning).

11. Have the lowest possible elapsed time per lap (ideal scene).

12. Have an understanding of what you did right (good control and better lap times).

13. Have an understanding of what you did wrong (what actions produced poor control or slower lap times).

Are you ready to improve your riding?

Chapter Recap

1. There are three ways to improve your riding:
   a) Lots of laps.
   b) Lots of thought.
   c) Lots of laps and lots of thoughts.

2. There are two ways to look at your riding, and two ways to change the things you're doing:
   a) Plan what you will spend your **attention** on.
   b) Plan where you will work the **controls** and in what order you will work them.

3. Going over how you spend your attention is the best and easiest way to discover what you were doing. Just trace back along your **attention line** to discover what you did.

4. The **5 senses** of riding are what occupy a rider's attention. They are:
   a) Location
   b) Traction
   c) Speed
   d) Lean Angle
   e) Timing

5. You begin to handle your riding by fixing the areas that give you trouble; they are the first things to adjust. Following back along your **attention line** is difficult in problem turns, and easy where you are doing well.

6. There are five reasons for not being able to easily recall what you did in a turn:
   a) Attention on too many things at once.
   b) Attention on the wrong thing.
   c) Attention out of sequence.
   d) Attention stuck on the controls.
   e) Too little attention on the controls.

7. **Attention** isn't only what you focus your eyes on. Your Sense of Traction, for instance, has nothing to do with eyesight.

8. When looking over an area of your riding you should pay close attention to whether the control actions you are performing are helping or hurting.
   a. The Idea that you should always get a drive at the exit of a turn could be wrong if it were bumpy or off camber.
   b. If the bike is sliding or pointed in the wrong direction, it is what you are doing with the controls that is making that happen.

9. The riders main resource in making a Plan is deciding where his Attention is best going to be spent. It is just like budgeting out your pay check.

10. You can spend your Attention in 2 areas:
    a. Maintaining the Motion of the bike.
    b. Investing it in Future Motion, things you will want to be happening later on in the turn.

11. Whether your riding has been carefully Planned out or not you can dissect it and decide on what should be done and what isn't important.
    a. Devising a Plan is nothing more than Planning out where you will spend your Attention.

12. The Sampling procedure has a lot to do with how you sense your riding.
    a. Not Sampling your Motion often enough, will give you the idea that everything is changing very fast.
    b. The more often you Sample something the less it appears to change.

13. Your Sense of Timing applies to spending your Attention wisely.
    a. Switching your Attention on the next thing too soon would start that action before you need it.
    b. Switching your Attention too late will put you behind time for the next thing you have to do.

14. There is a Force that you feel when the bike is steered into a turn. It is the result of the bike wanting to go straight and the rider changing that direction with the bars.
    a. The faster you turn, the greater the Force.
    b. The slower you turn the less the Force is.

15. The amount of Force you experience may be giving you false information about how fast you are entering turns.

16. The actual Speed of the bike is separate from that Force.
    a. The force is telling you how quickly you turned not how fast the bike is going.
    b. Your entry speed is far more important than this initial cornering Force.

17. To avoid using the Turning Force to get information on your speed, you only have to Plan and Decide to keep it on the Speed at that point in the turn, and realize that it is a false source of speed information.

18. Poor physical condition can contribute to rough riding. It isn't really because you aren't strong enough it is because your Attention goes over onto your body and that is the wrong place for it to be.

19. There are 13 points that must be considered or mastered before your riding is really under control.
    a. The 13 points state the Ideal situation a rider would have to be able to win and improve.

Start!

NOTES

CHAPTER XII

Confidence

A Winning Smile And One Thought In Mind.

Confidence is a word that means trust, faith, assurance and especially, self-assurance. It's generally agreed that an athlete should have some of it. Some racers have it by the truckload and some wear it on their faces as armor on raceday.

You can have it one lap and not the next. Without it, riding seems like labor and with it, it's a dream. What is it though? If you lose it, how do you get it back? If you've got it, how do you keep it? What happens to it after you've fallen down? Let's see.

I Can Do It..., Maybe.

With **confidence**, you go about your riding with the thoughts "to do it right," "to do it better," "different," "like someone else," or whatever. Your thoughts, feelings and ideas are **to do it**.

Occasionally, a **second thought** comes into play, usually just before you do something. Those thoughts are "What I don't want to do," "What I shouldn't do," "What I can't do," "It's not going to work," or "Is it really OK to do this?" and so on.

You are on the track and just about to act on one of the positive thoughts from #1 above. Your **attention** goes over onto one of the #2 thoughts. The follow through on that action is now based on the #2 thought. I'm sure you know what this is all about. It is the beginning of a mistake.

Example: You **know** you can get into a turn faster than you are doing it. You are positive because just after entering the turn you always find yourself going too slow.

Each time you come up to that turn you intend to go a bit faster and just at the last moment before you pitch it in, there is that other thought and it generates a feeling of uncertainty. Your **confidence** goes away.

Do you see the difference? You know it can be done but you begin to act on that **second thought** you are thinking. **It shakes your intention to do it**. You have to act on something and that second thought is right there. Uncertainty sets in because at the last moment you varied your plan to go that little bit faster — no **confidence** that it would work!

Confidence And Attention

A second thought can stop you from acting on your PLAN.

1st Thought

2nd Thought

?

What is confidence then? **Confidence is: Knowing you can keep your attention on the job, no matter what.**

That **second thought** switched your **attention** away from what you knew you could do, your **plan**. Think about it; if you can't keep your **attention** on what you are doing, you make mistakes and it is because of that **second thought** that comes in and switches your **attention** away from the job.

Crash Confidence

You can look back over a situation and figure it out. Some rider who crashed was in such and such a turn and something happened so that he began operating on his second idea of doing it wrong and then he does it wrong and falls down right at that instant or shortly after.

Now he's all healed up from that crash and trying to ride again and isn't quite sure if he crashed because of idea #1, **to do it by the plan**, or idea #2, **that he couldn't do it**. He's not sure and boy is that low **confidence**.

Maybe he was always doing it wrong and simply "getting away with it." You see? All of his **confidence** in what he could do is now under question!!!

153

World Confidence

When a world champion rider is helping someone out and says to him, "Just run it in until the front end pushes," what is he saying? Is he saying that because he doesn't know how to do it? **No**. He's saying, "You decide how fast you can get it in and then you operate on that idea with 100% **confidence**. It is going to push the front end and that is just a little too fast. You want to note that little fact and then back it off a little the next time you come into that turn, or just let it push."

Bravery Or Confidence

You have to be able to appreciate the point of view of someone who is totally committed to the idea that once a plan has been made you better not change it. You have to appreciate how unshakable this person must be to overcome all the temptations to change, and just continue to keep his **attention** on the job.

Of course, it isn't totally cut and dried. If something happens that isn't working or is leading to a crash, you are going to expect the world class rider to pull out one of his alternate plans, for not crashing, from his bag of tricks. There is a big difference between "casting your fate to the winds" and doing something with 100% confidence.

The difference is, the veteran acts, focusing the **attention** he has freed up by making his plan, and checking to see if his result is correct. He spends it on **sampling**. The novice rider spends his **attention** on forcing himself. **Do you see the difference**?

The pro has his extra **attention** focused on gathering information and the new guy has his **attention** fixed **inwardly**, on himself. That is a mistake.

Your Confidence

You can try to do something with the idea it will go right. You can try something with the idea it won't or might not. You cannot try it with both ideas at once.

Making DECISIONS keeps your ATTENTION free to ride.

Can you enter that turn as fast as you think you can? Yes? You're sure? Good.

What is the first thing that might happen if you're wrong? Will it push the front end or slide the rear, or both? Fine, it will do one of those things.

What will you do if that happens? Turn the throttle on, off, steer it wider, or turn it in more? You decide.

What will happen if it goes the way you thought it would? Have you thought out what will happen if you get it into that turn as fast as you think you can? If you haven't, how are you going to keep your **attention** on it? What is giving you the **confidence** to do it in the first place if you don't know what will happen?

The Best Laid Plans

The above are some important questions. If you are a really good rider, you can answer them even if you hadn't taken the time to think of them in the first place. They are things you would have worked out "naturally."

It brings up another part of **confidence**. If you have a plan worked out, it will take into account what will happen if you are right and what you will have to do if it isn't workable. That covers you whether right or wrong.

Example: "I know I can get into that turn faster." OK, what will happen if you do? You can go through the list of results from more speed: Running wider, harder to steer, loss of traction, or whatever applies to this turn.

Alright. "What if I get in too hot?" Is there room to let the bike go wide and scrub off some speed? Could you let it slide a little to scrub off the extra speed?

One of those will apply to the situation and if thought out beforehand you would have a plan for almost any result you came up with.

If you were already out of road or lean angle, it would be unwise to make that decision "to go in faster." At that point you would just be hoping for a miracle.

Confident Plans

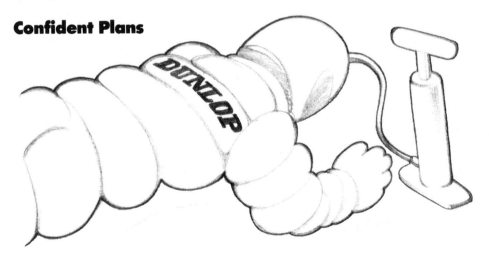

Pumping yourself up is no substitute for well planned riding.

155

When you come on an interesting part of the book, you relate it to a specific turn and that is a good refresher. You can learn from it.

Confidence is a result of having plans.

Some riders give you the idea that **confidence** is something manufactured in the pits by pumping yourself up and having steam roll off your helmet at the starting line. It's not, and it is a mistake to think it is.

It is the result of knowing you can keep your **attention** on the job, no matter what happens. It comes from knowledge and experience. It is not a product of adrenalin.

The opposite side of the coin is that you may need to pump yourself up some to go out and get your plans in order. If you are trying new stuff that requires you to do more or keep your attention on something new, you may just have to use "the pump."
Good Luck.

Chapter Recap

1. It is agreed that **confidence** is a necessary ingredient in winning and performing at your best.

2. **Confidence** can be shattered by the simple process of having a second idea come into play while you are riding, just at the moment you go into action to do something on the track.

3. This second thought or idea brings about the opposite of - **confidence — uncertainty.**

4. A working definition of **confidence** is: **Knowing you can keep your attention on the job, no matter what happens.**

5. Having another thought or idea can result in crashing. This can drop the rider's **confidence**. He may not remember which idea he was using at the time he crashed. It can get to him. He can become unsure of just exactly which idea or plan made him crash. He may have to go over all of his riding to discover the reason.

6. A world class rider uses his confidence to free up his attention so he can observe how his plan is working. The novice often uses the idea of **confidence** to become "brave."

7. Working out the possible results of your Plan will bring up your **confidence** just because you have spent time considering the results of something you want to try.

8. **Confidence** is a result. It is what you gain from being sure of your plans. It is not the result of pumping yourself up.

9. Pumping yourself up has its place. You may need to do it while you are trying new plans, but it is not the way to operate all the time.

Checklist:

1. Have you ever had a "second thought" while trying to do something on the track or while riding on the road, that led to a mistake?
2. Does that happen often?
3. Is there one particular thing that your attention goes to more than others?
    a) Does it go to speed: "I think this is too fast?"
    b) Does it go to traction: "I'm not sure it will stick?"
    c) Does it go to lean angle: "Am I over too far?"
    d) Does it go to location: "Where am I?"
    e) Does it go to timing: "Is it OK to roll it on, brake, etc?"
4. In the places you feel you are lacking in **confidence**:
    a) Do you have a plan?
    b) Is some other idea always coming up?
    c) Have you given up trying to get it right?
    d) Did you get it right once and then forget how?
    e) Are there several ideas on how to do it?
5. In a place you have a lot of **confidence**:
    a) Are you sure of your plan?
    b) Has the worst thing that could happen already occurred to you?
    c) Do you have spare attention in that place?
6. What would it take to feel that way in every turn?
7. How would your riding be if you did feel that way in every turn?
    a) Is that the way you want to ride?
    b) What is stopping you from doing it that way?
8. How long are you going to put up with the answers from #7b)?
    a) Will you handle them now or later?
You ought to do it now.

CHAPTER XIII

Troubleshooting Questionnaires

Answer The Questions And Stop That Torture You Call Riding.

Turn Classification

Maybe you aren't having any problems or think you don't but you can go over these questions and find the spots that need fixing.

1. Is the turn that's causing you trouble a:
   a) Slow turn?
   b) Medium-speed turn?
   c) Fast turn?
   d) Series of turns? (A chicane usually has three distinct steering changes, like at Daytona. An ess is usually two steering changes, like at Mid-Ohio, Sears Point or Riverside.)
   e) Downhill turn?
   f) Uphill turn?
   g) Crested turn?
   h) Combination of the above?

2. Does the turn have:
   a) Banked asphalt?
   b) Flat asphalt?
   c) Off-camber asphalt?
   d) Camber changes?
   e) Some combination of the above?

3. Is this turn:
   a) Decreasing-radius?
   b) Increasing-radius?
   c) Constant-radius?
   d) Part of a series with one or more of the above?

4. Does this turn have:
   a) Smooth asphalt?
   b) Bumpy asphalt?
   c) Part bumpy and part smooth asphalt?
   d) A particular bumpy part?

5. Is this a:
   a) Right turn?
   b) Left turn?

6. What area of the turn are you having trouble with:
   a) Entry?
   b) Middle?
   c) Exit?
   d) More than one part of it?

Overall Question Set For All Applications

It seems that you can only think about 5 things easily. This list will help.

1. Which control are you using?
   a) Brake lever?
   b) Throttle?
   c) Handlebars?
   d) Clutch?
   e) Shift Lever?
   f) More than one of the above?
2. What are you doing with that control?
   a) Working it hard?
   b) Working it gently?
   c) Can you change how you're using it while you're doing it?
   d) Are the controls easy to reach and use?
3. What is the result of using that control?
   a) What is the bike doing in response to your using that control?
   b) Is using a combination of controls causing any problems?
3a. Are you at the limit of the control you're using?
   a) Is the throttle all the way off?
   b) Is the throttle all the way on?
   c) Is the engine off the power and in the wrong gear?
   d) Is the engine at redline in the middle of the turn?
   e) Are you spinning the rear wheel from acceleration?
   f) Are you locking the front wheel from braking?
   g) Are you steering so hard the bike shakes?
   h) Is the bike leaned over all the way?
   i) Are you going so fast that you can't turn the bike where you want to?
   j) Are you locking up the rear wheel from downshifting?
   k) Are you locking up the rear wheel with the rear brake?
   l) Are you using the handlebars for leverage to change your body position?
4. Where does your attention go while using that control?
   a) What do you notice during that time?
   b) What are you thinking right then?
   c) What are you looking at right then?
5. Are you aware of what you're sampling right there?
   a) Traction?
   b) Speed?
   c) Lean Angle?
   d) Timing?
   e) Location?

5a. If you are **sampling traction**, is it:
  a) Currently available traction?
  b) Future traction you're trying to predict?
  c) Trying to find the traction limit (sense of traction)?
  d) Trying to remember previous traction (traction memory)?
  e) Getting the bike to stick or slide where you want it to (target traction)?

5b. If you are **sampling speed**, are you:
  a) Trying to reach a different speed than before (target speed)?
  b) Trying to get the same speed as before (speed memory)?
  c) Playing with the speed to see what works (sense of speed)?

5c. If you are **sampling lean angle**, are you:
  a) Trying to get a different lean angle than before (target lean angle)?
  b) Trying to get the same lean angle as before (lean angle memory)?
  c) Experimenting with the lean angle to see what works (sense of lean angle)?

5d. If you are **sampling timing**, is it:
  a) What you can do now (current timing)?
  b) What you will be able to do (future timing)?
  c) Trying to determine what should be done and where (sense of timing)?

5e. If you are **sampling location**, are you:
  a) Looking at where you are now (current location)?
  b) Looking at where you will be in a short time (future location)?
  c) Trying to figure out where you are now (sense of location)?

6. If you are making mistakes, are they:
  a) In speed changes?
  b) In steering changes?
  c) Both speed and steering?

6a. Is there any difficulty in keeping your attention on what's important?

6b. Do you "give up" and just go along for the ride at this point?

7. What is the "most important thing" right here on the track?
  a) Speed?
  b) Traction?
  c) Lean Angle?
  d) Timing?
  e) Location?
  (List the five points in order of importance.)

8. Where did you get your **idea** about what to do here?
  a) Experience?
  b) Someone else told you how to do it?
  c) You watched someone else do it?
  d) You have your own idea of how to do it?
  e) You don't have any ideas at all; you're just doing it?

9. Do you have a **plan** for riding this section or turn?
  a) Have you thought it out enough to know what to do?
  b) Did you make decisions about what to do?
  c) Can you imagine your plan working out?

d) Are there parts to the plan that don't seem to fit?

e) Does this plan include things you've never done before?

f) Are you having a problem because there is no plan?

g) Is this a problem because you never decided how to do it at all?

10. Are you relaxed at this part of the track?

a) Do you feel "frozen" on the controls?

b) Is your body stiff?

c) Are you hanging onto the bike very tightly?

d) Are you breathing?

e) What could you do to be relaxed at this part of the track?

f) Would it help to be relaxed here?

11. What is your **body position** at this place on the track?

a) Are you moving around on the bike?

b) Are you in position for the next thing you must do?

c) Are you "caught" between positions uncomfortably.

d) Are your leathers too tight or too loose?

e) Are you sticking on the seat when you try to move around?

f) Are the controls in the right place for your body position?

g) Are you changing your body position just to reach the controls?

h) Are there other problems with your body position?

Seating position is important for using the controls. A lot of guys don't fix them but I have to have the bike fit me just right or it is hard to ride really fast.

12. Do you have a good idea of where to **begin** what you are doing here? (You can only change the speed/steering.)

a) Does where you start this action change from one lap to the next?

b) Are you "stuck" on a place to perform this action and can't seem to change?

c) Do you need to have a beginning marker for this action?

d) Can you change what you are doing here so that it works no matter what?

13. Do you have a good idea where to **end** what you are doing here?

a) Does where you end it change from lap to lap?

b) Are you "stuck" on a place to end this action?

c) Do you need to have an ending marker for this action?

d) Do you have it figured out so that you can end it when needed each lap?

14. Is there a particular problem **passing** here?

a) Does your attention go on the rider at this place on the track?

b) Does the idea of passing change too many things to be able to do it?

c) Do you have an alternate way of getting through this part of the track?

15. What have you **changed** right here?

a) Did that change make things work better?

b) Did that change make things work worse?

c) Did your lap times improve?

d) Did your lap times worsen?

e) Are you unable to tell whether the change helped or not?

f) Are you hoping your ability to ride this section will improve with practice?

g) Should you leave this area alone and work on something else?

16. Are you unsure of what the **limit** is on what you are doing here?

    a) Is your attention stuck here because you don't know what the bike will do?

    b) Did you reach the limit once before and didn't like it?

    c) Are you unsure of how to find the limit safely?

    d) Are you afraid of crashing here?

    e) Is it really important to find the limit here?

17. Are you sure in your own mind how you will now handle this area?

    a) Did you change your mind about how it should be done?

    b) Are you still unsure you can handle it?

    c) Did you decide to leave it alone?

    d) Are you going to forget about it and see what happens?

    e) Do you need to ride it again and get more information?

    f) Were you right to begin with?

THE HOW-TO TRIO

GLOSSARY

Apex. 1. The highest inside point in a turn. 2. The point at which the rider comes the closest to the inside edge of the track is his apex.

Attention. 1. Focused awareness. 2. Directing the senses toward something known or not known. 3. The ability to focus in on some aspect of riding.

Blue Groove. 1. Where the usable portion of the track builds up a layer of used rubber that is blueish in appearance, with high traction.

Chicane. 1. A three-turn section of a track with each turn following immediately after one another. 2. A section added to a track for the purpose of slowing down the speed. Generally added on to a straight section of the track. 3. A chicane is really only one turn but, because of its placement off to one side of the straight, it becomes three turns.

Cushion, or **Cush.** 1. Same as Tacky. 2. The track has moisture in the dirt so that no rubber is being layed down; fresh dirt is being kicked up. Excellent traction.

Decision. 1. The result of thinking through a riding problem and coming up with a plan that is intended to solve that problem. 2. A decision is an idea that is translated into an intended motion by the rider to correct or improve an existing riding technique. 3. There is a process to making a decision that starts with the rider recording his sense impressions of riding — how it feels. The impressions, when reviewed, become thoughts about riding. The thoughts, when assembled, make an idea. A plan is the result of putting an idea or ideas together into a procedure. A decision is the intention to act on the plan.

Deep. 1. The idea of riding into a turn keeping the bike vertical and going straight, for as long as possible, before turning.

Drifting. 1. Same as loose.

Drive. 1. The point in the turn where acceleration begins. 2. The degree of acceleration used to exit a turn. 3. The point at which a noticeable amount of acceleration can be used in a turn. 4. For a rider, the drive ends when the bike is out of danger of sliding out from the combination of lean angle and acceleration.

Early Apex. 1. Coming the closest to the inside edge of the track before the actual highest point of the inside of that turn. 2. A point before the actual apex of a turn.

Early Entry. 1. Beginning to turn the bike at the earliest opportunity for the upcoming corner. 2. Steering into a turn gradually and starting it well back from the turn.

Entry. 1. Where the rider has decided the turn starts. 2. Where the rider begins to steer the bike for a turn.

Esses. 1. Two or more turns in succession, generally high speed and layed out in an elongated "S" shape.

Exit. 1. Where the turn begins to straighten out. 2. Usually where the acceleration begins, toward the end of the turn. 3. The point at which the rider sees his way clear to begin the drive out.

Groove. 1. That part of the track which has the best traction. 2. The usable racing line developed by riders using that section of the track. 3. Creating traction by packing down the dirt from repeatedly riding over a section of the track. 4. The section of track most ridden on. (The groove can be any traction characteristic that narrows down the portion of the track that is being used. On a relatively smooth track that is becoming slippery, the groove will move out to where the traction is, becoming wider and wider.)

Head Shake. 1. A mildly unstable condition of the motorcycle where the fork assembly rapidly rotates, side to side, but only a short distance,

High, High Line. 1. Further away from the inside of the track. 2. Closer to the outside edge of the track. 3. A high line would be one more to the center or outside of the track or usable race line.

Idea. 1. A more or less complete grasp of a situation and its parts. 2. An idea is generated from thoughts about something. 3. Usually a solution to a situation or problem.

Late Apex. 1. Coming the closest to the inside edge of the track past the actual highest point of the inside of that turn. 2. A point past the actual apex of a turn.

Low, Low, Line. 1. Close to the inside edge of the track. 2. More to the inside of the agreed-upon racing line.

Loose. 1. Not perfect traction and not sliding. 2. A condition of traction where the bike is dancing across the surface slightly but not changing direction dramatically. 3. A fairly predictable, intermittent traction condition that is controllable.

Line. 1. The general description of a rider's path of travel through a turn. 2. The result of how a rider sees a turn and directs it through the turn. 3. The exact location of the bike at any given point in a turn.

Marbles. 1. Loose dirt on top of harder-packed dirt that offers poor traction.

Middle. 1. The center portion of a turn. 2. The portion of a turn that starts after the steering is done and ends as the acceleration out of the turn begins.

Plan. 1. A procedure that the rider has decided upon. 2. The careful ordering of important riding actions that can be predicted. 3. Where a rider spends his attention and how long he leaves it on each action is really the plan whether he decides to do it that way or not.

Pointing. 1. The rider's actions that result in the bike going in the intended direction. Steering, sliding or a combination of the two bring about the desired direction of the bike, usually in conjunction with the drive out of the turn.

RP, (reference point). 1. An exact location the rider uses to judge his position on the track. 2. A known point or area that has some meaning, i.e., a place to perform some action, brake, turn, etc.

Sampling. 1. The action of sensing the motion of the machine, i.e., speed, handling, lean angle, traction, etc., then measuring the sense information against your own plan or idea of how it is supposed to be. 2. The shifting of attention from the motion to the thought, back and forth, in rapid succession. Sampling can be done as fast as the individual can switch his attention from one to the other.

Scrub Off. 1. To reduce the speed of a bike, in a turn, by not applying throttle. 2. To lean the bike over more than is necessary to reduce its speed. 3. To allow the cornering forces to act on the bike, to slow it down, without reversing that force by throttle action or bringing the bike to a more vertical position. 4. Widening the path of travel through a turn to give the bike more room to slow down.

Slick. 1. When the moisture in the track is coming up to the surface too fast. 2. An over-wet condition of the dirt. 3. Also, sometimes, an over-dry condition of the track. A dusty track can be slick as well but often the feel is better than with an over-wet condition. 4. A smooth dirt surface with rubber on it can be slippery.

Tank Slapper. 1. A rapid and excessive alternating motion of the handlebars along their arc of travel. 2. An unstable condition of the motorcycle wherein the bars come in close proximity to the tank. 3. The fork assembly going from one steering stop to the next in rapid succession (slapping), while the bike is in motion. (Generally accompanied by a sudden increase in heart rate.)

Target. 1. An exactly defined, short-term goal. 2. A desired result.

Wiggle. 1. An unstable condition of a motorcycle wherein the front and back are oscillating from side to side.